the MIRACLE MORNING

THE NOT-SO-OBVIOUS SECRET GUARANTEED TO TRANSFORM YOUR LIFE BEFORE 8AM

1st Edition

JOURNAL

ISBN 978-0-9790197-8-4   0-9790197-8-8
© 2013 Hal Elrod International
www.MiracleMorning.com

"The only thing I regret about journaling is that I waited so long to start."

—HAL ELROD

CONTENTS

This Miracle Morning Journal Belongs To.. 4

My Miracle Morning Journal Pledge.. 4

1. **A Special Invitation:** Join *The Miracle Morning* Community............... 5

2. **Introduction:** How To Use Your Miracle Morning Journal................... 6

3. **The Life S.A.V.E.R.S.** – Six Practices Guaranteed............................... 8
   To Save You From a Life of Unfulfilled Potential

4. **The 6-Minute Miracle Morning** (Because We All Get Busy)............... 45

5. *The Miracle Morning* **Journal Begins:** Week #1 of 52....................... 48

6. **Six-Month Review:** Capitalizing On Your 1st Half of the Year............... 100

7. **BONUS:** What You Must Do Now If You're Serious About 147
   Making the Next 12 Months Even Better ....

8. **Annual Review:** Lessons + New Commitments = Best Year Ever............ 159

This Miracle Morning Journal Belongs To:

Name _____

Address _____

_____

Phone _____

Fax _____

Email _____

Website/Blog _____

Twitter _____

My Miracle Morning Journal Pledge:

I, _____ _____ commit to writing in my *Miracle Morning* Journal each day because I know that doing so will provide me with enhanced clarity, heightened self-awareness, and an increased level of commitment to the goals, dreams, and miracles that I want to create for my life. If I miss a day (because I'm not always perfect and life throws curveballs at me sometimes), I promise to go back the following day and recall the significant events, lessons, and all that I'm grateful for, to complete my journal entry. I believe that I am just as worthy, capable and deserving of extraordinary health, happiness, wealth and success as any other person on earth, and from this day forward I will live in alignment with that truth.

Signature: _____ Date: _____

The Miracle Morning Community

Fans and readers of *The Miracle Morning* make up an extraordinary community of like-minded individuals who wake up each day *on purpose*, dedicated to fulfilling the unlimited potential that is within each of us. As creator of *The Miracle Morning*, it was my responsibility to create an online space where readers and fans could go to connect, get encouragement, share ideas, support one another, discuss the book, post videos, find an Accountability Partner, and even swap smoothie recipes and exercise routines.

Visit **www.MyTMMCommunity.com** to join *The Miracle Morning* Community of inspired, like-minded miracle makers and achievers. Here you can connect with others who are also practicing *The Miracle Morning*—many whom have been doing it for years—to get additional support on your journey.

I'll be moderating the Community and checking in regularly. I look forward to seeing you there!

If you'd like to connect with me on Twitter, follow **@HalElrod**, and on Facebook at **Facebook.com/YoPalHal**. Please feel free to send me a direct message, leave a comment, or ask me a question. I do my best to answer every single one, so let's connect soon!

With sincere gratitude,

"Yo Pal" Hal Elrod

How To Use Your
Miracle Morning Journal

Welcome! Congratulations on beginning the process of investing time each day to document the journey of your life, here in *The Miracle Morning* Journal. The following is a quick overview of how to use your Miracle Morning Journal to maximize its benefits & your results.

Your *Miracle Morning* Journal uses a daily, weekly, and yearly format, and is dated to keep you accountable to write in it every single day of the year. You'll also find sections to review your progress at the end of each week, halfway through the year, and again at the end of the year, to capitalize on your significant lessons and accomplishments.

√ **Daily:** Increase Your Self-Awareness... Every Day

Start writing in your MM Journal on a daily basis and soon it will become a habit that adds tremendous value to your life and takes little effort. *The Miracle Morning* journaling process is a proven way to program your conscious and subconscious minds for extraordinary levels of success while improving your self-concept immediately, and increasingly over time.

√ **Weekly:** Review, Learn, and Improve... Every Week

There is space in your MM Journal for a Weekly Review, to think back over your week, review your daily journal entries, and acknowledge both your accomplishments as well as any disappointments you may have had. You'll learn from both and become a better version of yourself as a result of your willingness to look honestly at both aspects of yourself and your life.

√ **The Life S.A.V.E.R.S.:** Track Your Progress Daily

If you've read *The Miracle Morning* book then you're well aware of the life-transforming benefits of the *Life S.A.V.E.R.S.* model for accelerated personal development. In case you have not yet read *The Miracle Morning* book, or in case you c— simply use a refresher, I've included an excerpt of the popu— chapter: *Life S.A.V.E.R.S.—Six Practices Guaranteed To Save Yo From a Life of Unfulfilled Potential.*

The final "S" in the *Life S.A.V.E.R.S.* stands for "Scribing" (my favorite form of which is journaling) and here is where I give additional tips on getting the most out of your *Miracle Morning* journaling process.

√ **The 6-Minute Miracle Morning**

If you ever feel busy—too busy to do some of the things that you *know* are good for you—you need to read the book excerpt I've also included here in your MM Journal: *The 6-Minute Miracle Morning* to show you how you can accomplish all six of the *Life S.A.V.E.R.S.* in as little as six minutes a day, while still gaining all of the profound benefits of each.

Final Thoughts

Remember, any time you are implementing a new habit, change, or routine, it almost always feels a little uncomfortable. If you are feeling a little anxious or apprehensive about beginning the journaling process, know that it's completely normal. In fact, if you are without apprehension, you may *not* be normal! (I mean that in a good way, of course.)

I'm sure you already know from experience that taking your first step is always the most difficult one to take, and then every step after that become easier and easier. So, take your first step NOW. You can start by reading the *Life S.A.V.E.R.S.*—and discovering the *Six Practices Guaranteed To Save You From a Life of Unfulfilled Potential.* Or you can flip directly to today's date and starting writing in your MM Journal (or both).

Either way, you're about to give yourself the gift of daily journaling, one of the most life-enhancing practices you'll ever experience. Let the miracles begin!

⇒ Excerpt from *The Miracle Morning*
The bestselling book by Hal Elrod

The Life S.A.V.E.R.S.

Six Practices Guaranteed To Save You From a Life of Unfulfilled Potential

---

Success is something you attract by the person you become.
—JIM ROHN

An extraordinary life is all about daily, continuous improvements in the areas that matter most.
—ROBIN SHARMA

Stressed. Overwhelmed. Frustrated. Unfulfilled. Blah.

These are a few unpleasant words that provide a rather unfortunate, but fairly accurate description of how the average person feels about his or her life, far too often.

You and I are undoubtedly living in one of the most prosperous, advanced times in human history, with more opportunities and resources available to us than ever before. Yet most of us aren't tapping into the unlimited potential that is within every single one of us. I'm not okay with that. Are you?

The Potential Gap

Have you ever felt like the life you want to live and the person you know you can be are just beyond your grasp? Do you ever feel like you're chasing your potential—you know it's there, you can see it—but you can never quite catch it? When you see people who are excelling in an area that you're not, does it seem like they've got it all figured out—like they must know something that you don't know, because if you knew *it*, then you'd be excelling in that area too?

8

Most of us live our lives on the wrong side of a huge gap potential, a gap which separates who we are from who we can bec We are often frustrated with ourselves, our lack of consis motivation, effort and results in one or more areas of life. We spend t much time *thinking* about the actions we should be taking to create th results that we want, but then we don't take those actions. We all know what we need to do; we just don't consistently do what we know. Can you relate?

This *potential gap* varies in size from person to person. You may feel like you're very near your current potential and that a few tweaks could make all the difference. Or you might feel the opposite—like your potential is so far away from who you've been that you don't even know where to start. Whatever the case is for you, know that it is absolutely possible and attainable for you to live your life on the right side of your potential gap and become the person you are capable of becoming.

Whether you are currently sitting on the wrong side of the grand canyon of your potential, wondering how you're going to get to the other side, or you've been working your way across the canyon but are stuck at a plateau and haven't been able to close that gap and get to the next level—this chapter will introduce you to six tools that will enable you to go from where you are—accepting less from yourself than what you know is possible— to developing yourself into the person you *know* you can become.

Your Life Is Not What You Think It Is

Most of us are so busy trying to manage, maintain, or even just survive our life "situation" that we don't make the time to focus on what's most important—our *life*. What's the difference? Our life situation is the set of *external* circumstances, events, people, and places that surround us. It's not who we are. We are more than our life situation.

Your *life* is who you are at the deepest level. Your life is made up of the *internal* components, attitudes, and mindsets that can give you the power to alter, enhance, or change your life situation at any given moment.

Your *life* is made up of the *Physical, Intellectual, Emotional,* and *Spiritual* parts that make up every human being—or *P.I.E.S.* for short. The *Physical* includes things like your body, health, and energy. The

9

ectual incorporates your mind, intelligence, and thoughts. The *tional* takes into account your emotions, feelings, and attitudes. The *ritual* includes intangibles such as your spirit, soul, and the unseen gher power that oversees all.

Your *life* is where your ability to create new feelings, perspectives, beliefs, and attitudes in your "inner" world lies, so that you can create or alter the circumstances, relationships, results, and anything else in the "external" realm of your life situation. As many sages have taught us: *our outer world is a reflection of our inner world.* In other words, by focusing time and effort each day on developing your *P.I.E.S.*, and constantly becoming a better version of yourself, your life situation will inevitably—almost automatically—improve.

I can assure you that through my own transformative journey—from the depths of mediocrity, justifying my excuses and living most areas of my life somewhere in-between mediocre and average, to achieving goals that at one time seemed impossible for me—your commitment to daily personal development will be as instrumental for your transformation as it was for mine.

Time To Save The Life You Deserve To Live

For too many people, the extraordinary, fulfilling abundant life that they really want—our *Level 10* life—eludes them because they're so overwhelmed and overrun with their day-to-day life situation. Their life situation is eating up all of their time so that their life, and what matters most, isn't getting attended to.

In order to save your *Level 10* life from being neglected and limited by the demands of your life situation—which ultimately leads to a life of regret, unfulfilled potential, and even mediocrity—you must prioritize and dedicate time each day to your personal development. Enter *The Miracle Morning Life S.A.V.E.R.S.*—a set of six simple, *life*-enhancing, *life*-changing daily practices, each of which develops one or more of the *physical, intellectual, emotional,* and *spiritual* aspects of your life, so that you can become who you need to be to create the life you want.

Remember, when you change your inner world—your *life*—then your outer world—your *life situation*—will improve in parallel.

The First "S" of S.A.V.E.R.S.

Nope, it's not "sleep." Sorry. While I know many people would love it if they could sleep their way to success, unless you have been cryogenically frozen and are awaiting a large inheritance at the time of being thawed out—life just doesn't work that way.

Here are six powerful, proven personal development practices known as the *Life S.A.V.E.R.S.* that you'll use to gain access to the powerful forces—already within you—that will enable you to alter, change, or transform any area of your life. Let's look at each of the six personal development tools that make up the *Life S.A.V.E.R.S.* and how each will help you become the person you need to be to easily attract, create, and live the most extraordinary life you have ever imagined.

Life S.A.V.E.R.S.

S is for Silence

In the attitude of silence the soul finds the path
in a clearer light, and what is elusive and deceptive
resolves itself into crystal clearness.
—MAHATMA GANDHI

You can learn more in an hour of silence
than you can in a year from books.
—MATTHEW KELLY

Silence is the first practice of the *Life S.A.V.E.R.S.* and may be one of the most significant areas for improvement for our noisy, fast-paced and over-stimulated lifestyles. I'm referring to the life-transforming power of *purposeful Silence.* "Purposeful" simply means that you are engaging in a period of Silence with a highly beneficial purpose in mind—not just for the heck of it. As Matthew Kelly so eloquently states in his bestselling book *The Rhythm of Life*, "You can learn more in an hour of silence than you can in a year from books." That's a powerful statement from a very wise man.

If you want to immediately reduce your stress levels, to begin each day with the kind of calm, clarity, and peace of mind that will allow you to stay focused on what's most important in your life, and even dance on the edge of enlightenment—do the opposite of what *most people* do— start every morning with a period of purposeful Silence.

The life-enhancing benefits of Silence have been well documented throughout the ages. From the power of prayer, to the magic of meditation, some of the greatest minds in history have used purposeful Silence to transcend their limitations and create extraordinary results.

How Do Your Mornings Usually Begin?

Do you invest time in centering yourself and creating an optimum state of mind to lead you through the rest of the day? Or do you usually wait to wake up until you've got something to do? Do the words *calm, peaceful,* or *rejuvenating* describe your average morning? If they do, congratulations! You're already a step ahead of the rest of us.

For most of us, words like *rushed, hectic, stressful* or even *chaotic* might best describe our typical morning. For others, *slow, lazy,* and *lethargic* might be a more accurate description of how the morning begins. Which of these scenarios best describes your average morning?

Mornings, for most of us, are typically pretty hectic and rushed. We're usually running around trying to get ready for the day, and our minds are often plagued with internal chatter about *what we have to do, where we have to go, who we have to see, what we forgot to do, the fact that we're running late, a recent argument with our significant other or family member.*

For others, we have trouble just getting going on most mornings. We feel sluggish, lazy, and unproductive. So, for the great majority of us, the mornings are either stressful and rushed, or slow and unproductive. Neither of these represents the optimum way to start your day.

Silence is one of the best ways to immediately reduce stress, while increasing your self-awareness and gaining the clarity that will allow you to maintain your focus on your goals, priorities, and what's most important for your life, each and every day.

Here are some of my favorite activities to choose from and practice during my period of Silence, in no particular order, followed by a simple meditation to get you started:

√ Meditation
√ Prayer
√ Reflection
√ Deep Breathing
√ Gratitude

Some mornings I do just one of these activities, and other mornings I combine them. All of these practices will relax your mind and body,

13

calm your spirit, and allow you to be totally present and open to receiving the benefits that will come from the remaining *Life S.A.V.E.R.S.* which make up the rest of your *Miracle Morning*.

It is very important that you don't stay in bed for this, and preferably that you leave your bedroom altogether. The problem with staying in bed—or even in your bedroom, where your comfy bed is within your line of sight—is that it's too easy to go from *sitting* in Silence, to slouching, to falling back asleep. I always sit on my living room couch, where I already have everything set up that I need for my *Miracle Morning*. My affirmations, journal, yoga DVD, the book I'm currently reading—everything has its place and is ready for me each day so that, in the morning, it's easy to jump right in and engage in my *Miracle Morning*, without having to search for anything.

Meditation

Since there are plenty of great books, articles, and websites that concentrate on meditation, I won't go into too much detail in describing the proven benefits and the various approaches to meditating. Instead, I'll just mention a few of what I believe are the most significant benefits, and give you simple step-by-step meditation that you can begin immediately.

The essence of meditation is simply silencing or focusing the mind for a period of time. You may or may not be aware of all the extraordinary health benefits of meditating. Study after study shows that meditation can be more effective than *medication.* Studies link regular meditation to changes in metabolism, blood pressure, brain activation, and other mind and bodily functions. It can alleviate stress and pain, promote sleep, enhance focus and concentration, and even increase lifespan. Meditation also requires very little time. You can take advantage of the benefits of meditation in just a few minutes a day.

Well known celebrities, CEOs and highly successful people like Jerry Seinfeld, Sting, Russell Simmons, Oprah and many more have publically stated that regular, often daily, meditation has become an invaluable part of their life. Tupperware® CEO Rick Goings told *The Financial Times* that he tried to meditate for at least 20 minutes every day, stating, "For me, it's a practice that not only burns off stress, but gives me fresh eyes to clarify what's really going on and what really matters." Oprah told Dr. Oz that Transcendental Meditation® has helped her "connect with that which is God," according to the *Huffington Post.*

There are many genres and types of meditation, but generally speaking you can divide them into two categories: "guided" and "individual" meditations. Guided meditations are those in which you listen to another person's voice and receive instructions to help guide your thoughts, focus, and awareness. Individual meditations are simply those you do on your own, without assistance from anyone else.

Miracle Morning Meditation

For exclusive access to *Miracle Morning* guided meditations which I created specifically for you to use during your *Miracle Morning*, take a moment to download the brand new *Miracle Morning* **iPhone/iPad App** (also compatible with Android)—available now in the app store.

Otherwise, here is a simple, step-by-step individual meditation that you can use during your *Miracle Morning*, even if you've never meditated before.

• Before beginning your meditation, it's important to prepare your mindset and set your expectations. This is a time for you to quiet your mind and let go of the compulsive need to constantly be *thinking* about something—either reliving the past, stressing or worrying about the future—but never living fully in the present. This is the time to let go of your stresses, take a break from worrying about your problems, and be fully present in *this* moment. It is a time to access the essence of who you *truly* are—to go deeper than what you have, what you do, or the labels you've accepted as "who you are"—which most people have never even attempted to do. Accessing this essence of *who you truly are* is often referred to as "just being." Not thinking, not doing, just *being.* If this sounds foreign to you, or too "new-agey" that's okay. I used to feel the same way. It's probably just because you've never tried it before. But thankfully, you're about to.

• Find a quiet, comfortable place to sit. You can sit up straight on the couch, on a chair, on the floor, or sit on a pillow, for added comfort.

• Sit upright, cross-legged. You can close your eyes, or you can look down at the ground, approximately two feet in front of you.

- Begin by focusing on your breath, taking slow, deep breaths. In through the nose, out through the mouth, and be sure to breathe into your belly, rather than your chest. The most effective breathing should cause your belly to expand, and not your chest.

- Now, start pacing your breath; in slowly on a count of 3 seconds (one, one-thousand, two, one-thousand, three, one-thousand)... hold it in for 3 seconds (one, one-thousand, two, one-thousand, three, one-thousand)... and then breathe out slowly on a count of 3 seconds (one, one-thousand, two, one-thousand, three, one-thousand). Feel your thoughts and emotions settling down as you focus on your breath. Be aware that as you attempt to quiet your mind, thoughts will still come in to pay a visit. Simply acknowledge them, then let them go, always returning your focus to your breath.

- Remember, this is a time for you to let go of your compulsive need to constantly be *thinking* about something. This is a time to let go of your stress and take a break from worrying about your problems. This is the time to be fully present in *this* moment. This is often referred to as just *being*. Not thinking, not doing, just being. Continue to follow your breaths, and imagine inhaling positive, loving, peaceful energy, and exhaling all of your worries and stress. Enjoy the quiet. Enjoy the moment. Just breathe... *Just be.*

- If you find that you have a constant influx of thoughts, it may be helpful for you to focus on a single word or a phrase, and repeat it over and over again to yourself, as you inhale and exhale. For example, you might try something like: (On the inhale) "I breathe in peace..." (As you exhale) "I breathe out love... I breathe in peace..." (inhale)... "I breathe out love..." (exhale)... You can swap the words *peace* and *love* with whatever you feel like you need bring more of into your life (confidence, faith, belief, etc.), and whatever you feel like you want to give more of to the world.

- Meditation is a gift you can give to yourself every day. It truly is an incredible gift. My time spent meditating has become one of my favorite parts of my day. It is a time to be at peace, to experience gratitude, and a time of freedom from our day-to-day stressors and worries. Think of daily meditation as a temporary vacation from your problems. While your problems will still be there when you finish your daily meditation, you'll find that you are much more centered and better equipped to solve them.

Final Thoughts On Silence

There's no single right way to spend time in Silence. You can pray, meditate, focus on what you're grateful for, or even engage in deep thought. For me, sitting in Silence—especially meditating—was at first rather difficult, probably because I have what doctors have diagnosed as ADHD. I don't know that I agree with their diagnosis or even with the idea that ADHD is a "disorder" (that's another conversation for another time), but I can attest that it's definitely a challenge for me to sit still and quiet my mind. Thoughts tend to race in and out, bouncing around like a pinball, almost nonstop.

So even though I would *sit* in Silence, my mind didn't stop racing. The fact that sitting still and clearing my mind was so difficult for me was precisely the reason why I had to commit to mastering it. It took me three or four weeks of practicing Silence every day before I felt competent. I got to a place where I would allow thoughts to come in, I'd peacefully acknowledge them, and then quietly let them drift away without getting frustrated. So don't be discouraged if spending time in Silence, or meditating, is at first a challenge for you.

As for how long to do your period of purposeful Silence, I recommend starting with five minutes, although in the next chapter I'll teach you how you can experience the life-enhancing benefits of Silence in as little as 60 seconds a day! When I began this practice, I'd sit in Silence, calm and relaxed, say a prayer, meditate, ponder what I was grateful for, and just breathe deeply, for five minutes. It's such a peaceful, perfect way to start each day.

Life S.**A**.V.E.R.S.

A is for Affirmations

It's the repetition of affirmations that leads to belief. Once that
belief becomes a deep conviction, things begin to happen.
—MUHAMMAD ALI

You will be a failure, until you impress the subconscious with
the conviction you are a success. This is done by making an affirmation,
which clicks.
—FLORENCE SCOVEL SHINN

"**I** am the greatest!" Muhammad Ali affirmed these words over and over again—and then he *became* them. Affirmations are one of the most effective tools for quickly becoming the person you need to be to achieve everything you want in your life. Affirmations allow you to design and then develop the mindset (thoughts, beliefs, focus) that you need to take any area of your life to the next level.

It is no coincidence that some of the most successful people in our society—celebrities like Will Smith, Jim Carrey, Suze Orman, Muhammad Ali, Oprah, and many more—have all been vocal about their belief that positive thinking and the use of affirmations has helped them on their journey to success and wealth.

Whether or not you realize it, incessantly talking to one's self is not just for crazy people. Every single one of us has an internal dialogue that runs through our heads, almost non-stop. Most of it is unconscious, that is, we don't consciously choose the dialogue. Instead, we allow our past experiences—both good and bad—to replay over and over again. Not only is this completely normal, it is one of the most important processes for each of us to learn about and master. Yet, very few people take responsibility for actively choosing the think positive, proactive thoughts that will add value to their lives.

I recently read a statistic that 80% of women have self-deprecating thoughts about themselves (body image, job performance, other people's opinion of them, etc.) throughout the day. I'm sure that men do also, although it may be to a lesser extent.

Your self-talk has dramatic influence on your level of success in every aspect of your life—confidence, health, happiness, wealth, relationships, etc. Your affirmations are either working for or against you, depending on how you are using them. If you don't consciously design and choose your affirmations you are susceptible to repeating and reliving the fears, insecurities, and limitations of your past.

However, when you actively design and write out your affirmations to be in alignment with what you want to accomplish and who you need to be to accomplish it—and commit to repeating them daily (ideally *out loud*)—they immediately make an impression on your subconscious mind. Your affirmations go to work to transform the way you think and feel so you can overcome your limiting beliefs and behaviors and replace them with those you need to succeed.

How Affirmations Changed My Life

My first real-life exposure to the power of affirmations came when I was living with one of my most successful friends, Matt Recore. Nearly every day, I would hear Matt shouting from the shower in his bedroom. Thinking he was yelling for me, I would approach his bedroom door, only to find that he was shouting things like, "I am in control of my destiny! I deserve to be a success! I am committed to doing everything I must do today to reach my goals and create the life of my dreams!" *What a weirdo*, I thought.

The only previous exposure I had to affirmations was through a popular 1990s spoof on the hit TV show *Saturday Night Live*, in which Al Franken's character Stuart Smalley used to stare into a mirror and repeat to himself, *"I'm good enough, I'm smart enough, and doggone it, people like me!"* As a result, I always thought of affirmations as a joke. Matt knew better. As a student of Tony Robbins, Matt had been using affirmations and incantations for years to create extraordinary levels of success. Owning five homes, and one of the top network engineers in the country (all by age 25), I should have figured Matt knew what he was doing. After all, I was the one renting a room in *his* house. Unfortunately, it took me a few more years to realize that affirmations were one of the most powerful tools for transforming your life.

My first first-hand experience using affirmations came when I read about them in Napoleon Hill's legendary book, *Think and Grow Rich* (which I highly recommend, by the way). Although I was skeptical that the repetition of affirmations was really going to make any measurable impact on my life, I thought I would give it a shot. If it worked for Matt, it might work for me. I chose to target the limiting belief I had developed after suffering significant brain damage in my car accident: *I have a horrible memory.*

If you read my first book, *Taking Life Head On!*, you know that my short-term memory was almost non-existent following my car accident. While this led to some pretty comical incidents, my memory was so poor that friends and family would spend hours visiting with me at the hospital, take a quick lunch break, and then return to have me greet them as if I hadn't seen them in years.

Facing such a real physical limitation due to a traumatic brain injury caused me to constantly reinforce the belief that *I have a horrible memory.* Anytime someone asked me to remember or remind them of something, I would always respond, "I would, but I really can't—I have brain damage and a horrible short-term memory."

It had been 7 years since my car accident, and while this belief was based on my reality *then*, it was time to let it go. Maybe my memory was so *horrible*, at least in part, because I had never made the effort to believe it could improve. As Henry Ford said, "Whether you think you can, or you think you can't, you're right either way."

If affirmations could change what was, to me, the most *justified* limiting belief that I had, then they could probably change anything. So, I created my first affirmation which read: *I am letting go of the limiting belief that I have a horrible memory. My brain is a miraculous organism capable of healing itself, and my memory can improve, but only in proportion to how much I believe it can improve. So, from this moment on, I am maintaining the unwavering belief that I have an excellent memory, and it's continuing to get better every day.*

I read this short affirmation every day, during my *Miracle Morning*. Still programmed with my past beliefs, I wasn't sure it was working. Then, two months after my first day reciting my affirmation, something occurred that hadn't occurred in over seven years. A friend asked me to *remember* to call her the next day, and I responded, "Sure, no problem." As soon as the words left my mouth, my eyes widened and I got excited! My limiting belief about my horrible memory was losing its power. I had replaced it and reprogrammed my subconscious mind with my new, empowering belief, using my affirmations.

From that point on, having also added the belief that *affirmations really work*, not only did my memory continue to improve, but I created affirmations for every area of my life that I wanted to advance. I began using affirmations to improve my health, finances, relationships, overall happiness, confidence, as well as any and all *beliefs*, *mindsets* and *habits* that needed an upgrade. Nothing was off-limits. There are no limits!

How's Your Programming?

We've all been programmed—at the sub-conscious level—to think, believe, and act the way we do. Our programming is a result of many influences, including what we have been told by others, what we have told ourselves, and all of our life experiences—both good and bad. Some of us have programming that makes it easy for us to be happy and successful, while others—possibly the majority—have programming that makes life difficult.

So, the *bad news* is that if we don't actively change our programming, our potential will be crushed and our lives limited by the fears, insecurities, and limitations of our past. We must stop programming ourselves for a life of mediocrity by focusing on what we're doing wrong, being too hard on ourselves when we make mistakes, and causing ourselves to feel guilty, inadequate, and undeserving of the success we really want.

The *good news* is that our programming can be changed or improved at any time. We can reprogram ourselves to overcome all of our fears, insecurities, bad habits, and any self-limiting, potential-destroying beliefs and behaviors we currently have, so we can become as successful as we want to be, in any area of our lives we choose.

You can use affirmations to start programming yourself to be confident and successful in everything you do, simply by repeatedly telling yourself who you want to be, what you want to accomplish and how you are going to accomplish it. With enough repetition, your subconscious mind will begin to believe what you tell it, act upon it, and eventually manifest it in your reality.

Putting your affirmations in writing makes it possible for you to choose your new programming so it moves you toward that desired condition or state of mind by enabling you to consistently review it. Constant repetition of an affirmation will lead to acceptance by the mind, and result in changes in your thoughts, beliefs and behaviors. Since you get to choose and create your affirmations, you can design them to help you establish the thoughts, beliefs, and behaviors that you want and need to succeed.

5 Simple Steps To Create Your Own Affirmations

Here are 5 simple steps to create your first affirmation, followed by a link where you can download free *Miracle Morning* affirmations:

Step 1: What You Really Want

The purpose of a written affirmation is to program your mind with the beliefs, attitudes, and behaviors/habits that are vital to your being able to attract, create, and to sustain your ideal levels of success—*Level 10* success—in every area of your life. So, your affirmation must first clearly articulate exactly what you want your ideal life to be like, in each area.

You can organize your affirmations according to the areas that you most want to focus on improving, such as Health/Fitness, Mindset, Emotions, Finances, Relationships, Spirituality, etc. Begin with clarifying, in writing, what you really want—your ideal vision for yourself and your life—in each area.

Step 2: Why You Want It

As my good friend Adam Stock, President of *Rising Stock, Inc.* once told me, "The wise begin with *why*s." Everyone wants to be happy, healthy, and successful, but wanting is rarely an effective strategy for getting. Those who overcome the temptations of mediocrity and achieve everything they want in life have an extraordinarily compelling *why* that drives them. They have defined a clear life purpose that is more powerful than the collective sum of their petty problems and the countless obstacles they will inevitably face, and they wake up each day and work toward their purpose.

Include why, at the deepest level, all of the things you want are important to you. Being crystal clear on your deepest *whys* will give you an unstoppable purpose.

Step 3: Whom You Are Committed To *Being* To Create It

As my first Coach, Jeff Sooey used to say, *this is where the rubber meets the road.* In other words, your life gets better only *after* you get better. Your outer world improves only after you've invested countless hours improving yourself. *Being* (who you need to be) and *doing* (what you need to do) are prerequisites for *having* what you want to have. Get clear on who you need to be, are *committed* to being, in order to take your life, business, health, marriage, etc. to the next level and beyond.

Step 4: What You're Committed To *Doing* To Attain It

Which actions will you need to take on a consistent basis to make your vision for your ideal life a reality? Want to lose weight? Your affirmation might say something like: *I am 100% committed to going to the gym 5 days a week and running on the treadmill for a minimum of 20 minutes.* If you're a salesperson, your affirmation might read: *I'm committed to making 20 prospecting calls every day, from 8am-9am.* The more specific your actions are, the better. Be sure to include frequency (how often), quantity (how many), and precise time frames (what times you'll begin and end your activities.)

It's also important to start small. If you're going to the gym 0 days a week for 0 minutes, going to 5 days a week for 20 minutes is a big leap. It's important to take manageable steps. Feel small successes along the way so you feel good and don't get discouraged by setting expectations too high to be able to maintain. You can build up to your ideal goal. Start by writing down a daily or weekly goal and decide when you will increase it. After a few weeks of successfully meeting your goal of going to the gym 2-days-a-week for 20 minutes, then move it up to 3-days-a-week for 20 minutes, and so on.

Step 5: Add Inspirational Quotes and Philosophies.

I am always on the lookout for quotes and philosophies that I can add to my affirmations. For example, one of my affirmations comes from the book *What Got You Here Won't Get You There* by Marshal Goldsmith. It reads, *"The #1 skill of influencers is the sincere effort to make a person feel that he or she is the most important person in the world. It's one of the skills that Bill Clinton, Oprah Winfrey, and Bruce Goodman used to become the best in their fields. I will do this for every person I connect with!"*

Another reads: *"Follow Tim Ferris' advice: To maximize productivity, schedule 3-5 hour blocks or half-days of singularly focused attention on ONE single activity or project, rather than trying to switch tasks every 60 minutes."*

Anytime you see or hear a quote that inspires you, or come across an empowering philosophy or strategy and think to yourself: *Man, that is a* **huge** *area of improvement for me*, add it to your affirmations. By focusing on these every day, you will begin to integrate the empowering philosophies and strategies into your way of thinking and living, which will improve your results and quality of life.

Final Thoughts On Affirmations

- In order for your affirmations to be effective, it is important that you tap into your emotions while reading them. Mindlessly repeating a phrase over and over again, without *feeling* its truth, will have a minimal impact on you. You must take responsibility for generating authentic emotions and powerfully infusing those emotions into every affirmation you repeat to yourself. Have fun with it. If you're excited about an affirmation, it doesn't hurt to dance and shout it from the rooftops!

- It can also be beneficial to incorporate a purposeful *physiology*, such as reciting your affirmations while standing tall, taking deep breaths, making a fist, or exercising. Combining physical activity with affirmations is a great way to harness the power of the mind-body connection.

- Keep in mind that your affirmations will never really be a "final" draft, because you should always be updating them. As you continue to learn, grow, and evolve, so should your affirmations. When you come up with a new goal, dream, habit, or philosophy you want to integrate into your life, add it to your affirmations. When you accomplish a goal or completely integrate a new habit into your life, you might find it's no longer necessary to focus on it every day, and thus choose to remove it from your affirmations.

- Finally, you must be consistent with reading your *daily* affirmations. That's right, you must read them daily. Saying an occasional affirmation is as effective as getting an occasional workout. You won't see any measurable results until you make them a part of your daily routine. That's largely what *The Miracle Morning 30-Day Life Transformation Challenge* (in Chapter 9) is all about—making each of the *Life S.A.V.E.R.S.* a habit so you can do them effortlessly.

- *One more thing to consider:* reading this book—or any book—*is* an affirmation to yourself. Anything you read influences your thoughts. When you consistently read positive self-improvement books and articles, you are programming your mind with the thoughts and beliefs that will support you in creating success.

Visit www.TMMbook.com to:

- Get help creating and perfecting your affirmations...
- See a sample of my own personal affirmations...
- View and download highly effective *Miracle Morning* affirmations on everything from *losing weight, improving your relationships, increasing your energy, developing extraordinary self-confidence, making more money, overcoming depression,* and much more...

V is for Visualization

Ordinary people believe only in the possible. Extraordinary
people visualize not what is possible or probable, but rather what
is impossible. And by visualizing the impossible, they
begin to see it as possible.
—CHERIE CARTER-SCOTT

See things as you would have them be instead of as they are.
—ROBERT COLLIER

Visualization, also known as *creative visualization* or *mental rehearsal*, refers to the practice of seeking to generate positive results in your outer world by using your imagination to create mental pictures of specific behaviors and outcomes occurring in your life. Frequently used by athletes to enhance their performance, visualization is the process of imagining exactly what you want to achieve or attain, and then mentally rehearsing what you'll need to do to achieve or attain it.

Many highly successful individuals, including celebrities, have advocated the use of visualization, claiming that it's played a significant role in their success. Such stars include Bill Gates, Arnold Schwarzenegger, Anthony Robbins, Tiger Woods, Will Smith, Jim Carey, and yet again, the one and only, Oprah. (Hmm… could there be a link between Oprah being one of the successful women in the world, and the fact that she practices most, if not *all* six of the *Life S.A.V.E.R.S.?*)

Tiger Woods, arguably the greatest golfer of all time, is famous for using visualization to mentally rehearse perfectly execution of his golf swing on every hole. Another world champion golfer, Jack Nicklaus, has said: "I never hit a shot, not even in practice, without having a very sharp in-focus picture of it in my head."

Will Smith stated that he used visualization to overcome challenges, and visualized his success years before actually becoming successful. Another famous example is actor Jim Carrey, who wrote himself a check in 1987 in the amount of 10 million dollars. He dated it for "Thanksgiving 1995" and added in the memo line, "For acting services rendered." He then visualized it for years, and in 1994 he was paid 10 million dollars for his starring role in *Dumb and Dumber*.

What Do You Visualize?

Most people are limited by visions of their past, replaying previous failures and heartbreaks. Creative Visualization enables you to design the vision that will occupy your mind, ensuring that the greatest pull on you is your *future*—a compelling, exciting, and limitless future.

Here's a brief summary of how I use Visualization, followed by three simple steps for you to create your own Visualization process. After I've read my affirmations, I sit upright on my living room couch, close my eyes, and take a few slow, deep breaths. For the next five minutes, I simply visualize myself living my ideal day, performing all of my tasks with ease, confidence, and enjoyment.

For example, during the months that I spent writing this book (okay, who am I kidding—it took *years*), I would first visualize myself writing with ease, enjoying the creative process, free from stress, fear, and writer's block. I also visualized the end result—people reading the finished book, loving it and telling their friends about it. Visualizing the process being enjoyable, free from stress and fear, motivated me to take action and overcome procrastination.

3 Simple Steps For Miracle Morning Visualization

Directly after reading your affirmations—where you took the time to articulate and focus on your goals and who you need to be to take your life to the next level—is the prime time to visualize yourself living in alignment with your affirmations.

Step 1: Get Ready

Some people like to play instrumental music in the background—such as classical or baroque (check out anything from the composer

Bach)—during their visualization. If you'd like to experiment with playing music, put it on with the volume relatively low.

Now, sit up tall, in a comfortable position. This can be on a chair, couch, floor, etc.

Breathe deeply.

Close your eyes, clear your mind, and get ready to visualize.

Step 2: Visualize What You Really Want

Many people don't feel comfortable visualizing success and are even scared to succeed. Some people may experience resistance in this area. Some may even feel guilty that they will leave the other 95% behind when they become successful.

This famous quote from Marianne Williamson's bestselling book, *A Return To Love,* may resonate with anyone who feels mental or emotional obstacles when attempting to visualize: "Our deepest fear is not that we are inadequate. Our deepest fear is that we are powerful beyond measure. It is our light, not our darkness that most frightens us. We ask ourselves, Who am I to be brilliant, gorgeous, talented, fabulous? Actually, who are you *not* to be? You are a child of God. Your playing small does not serve the world. There is nothing enlightened about shrinking so that other people won't feel insecure around you. We are all meant to shine, as children do. We were born to make manifest the glory of God that is within us. It's not just in some of us; it's in everyone. And as we let our own light shine, we unconsciously give other people permission to do the same. As we are liberated from our own fear, our presence automatically liberates others."

The greatest gift we can give to the people we love is to live to our full potential. What does that look like for you? What do you *really* want? Forget about logic, limits, and being practical. If you could have *anything* you wanted, do anything you wanted, and be anything you wanted—what would you have? What would you do? What would you be?

Visualize your major goals, deepest desires, and most exciting, would-totally-change-my-life-if-I-achieved-them dreams. See, feel, hear, touch, taste, and smell every detail of your vision. Involve all of your senses to maximize the effectiveness of your visualization. The more vivid you make your vision, the more compelled you'll be to take the necessary actions to make it a reality.

Now, fast forward into the future to see yourself achieving your ideal outcomes and results. You can either look toward the near future—the end of the day—or further into the future, like I did while writing this book, when I visualized people reading it, loving it, and recommending it to their friends. The point is you want to see yourself accomplishing what you set out to accomplish, and you want to *experience* how good it will feel to have followed through and achieved your goals.

Step 3: Visualize Who You Need To Be and What You Need To Do

Once you've created a clear mental picture of what you want, begin to visualize yourself living in total alignment with the person you need to be to achieve your vision. See yourself engaged in the positive actions you'll need to do each day (exercising, studying, working, writing, making calls, sending emails, etc.) and make sure you see yourself enjoying the process. See yourself smiling as you're running on that treadmill, filled with a sense of pride for your self-discipline to follow through. Picture the look of determination on your face as you confidently, persistently make those phone calls, work on that report, or finally take action and make progress on that project you've been putting off for far too long. Visualize your co-workers, customers, family, friends, and spouse responding to your positive demeanor and optimistic outlook.

Final Thoughts On Visualization

In addition to reading your affirmations every morning, doing this simple visualization process every day will turbo-charge the programming of your subconscious mind for success. You will begin to live in alignment with your ideal vision and make it a reality.

Visualizing your goals and dreams is believed by some experts to attract your visions into your life. Whether or not you believe in the *law of attraction*, there are practical applications for visualization. When you visualize what you want, you stir up emotions that lift your spirits and pull you toward your vision. The more vividly you see what you want, and the more intensely you allow yourself to experience *now* the feelings you will feel once you've achieved your goal, the more you make the possibility of achieving it feel real.

When you visualize daily, you align your thoughts and feelings with your vision. This makes it easier to maintain the motivation you need to continue taking the necessary actions. Visualization can be a powerful aid to overcoming self-limiting habits such as procrastination, and to taking the actions necessary to achieve your goals

I recommend starting with just five minutes of visualization. However, in the next chapter *The 6-minute Miracle Morning* I'm going to teach you how you can gain the powerful benefits of visualizing in just one minute per day.

[TMM Bonus] Create Your Vision Board

Vision Boards were made popular by the bestselling book and film *The Secret*. A Vision Board is simply a poster board on which you post images of what you want to have, who you want to become, what you want to do, where you want to live, etc.

Creating a Vision Board is a fun activity you can do on your own, with a friend, your significant other, or even your kids. It gives you something tangible to focus on during your Visualization. If you'd like detailed instructions on this process, Christine Kane has an excellent blog on *How To Make A Vision Board* as well as a free eBook titled *The Complete Guide To Vision Boards*. Both are available on her website at www.ChristineKane.com.

Keep in mind that, although creating a Vision Board is fun, nothing changes in your life without action. I have to agree with Neil Farber, M.D., Ph.D., who stated in his article on psychologytoday.com, "Vision boards are for dreaming, action boards are for achieving." While looking at your vision board every day may increase your motivation and help you stay focused on your goals, know that only taking the necessary actions will get you real-time results.

Life S.A.V.**E**.R.S.

E is for Exercise

If you don't make time for exercise, you'll probably
have to make time for illness.
—ROBIN SHARMA

The only exercise most people get is jumping to
conclusions, running down their friends, sidestepping
responsibility, and pushing their luck.
—UNKNOWN

Morning exercise should be a staple in your daily rituals. When you exercise for even a few minutes every morning it significantly boosts your energy, enhances your health, improves self-confidence and emotional well-being, and enables you to think better and concentrate longer. Too busy for exercise? In the next chapter, I'll show you how to fit in a workout every day—in as little as *60 seconds.*

I recently saw an eye-opening video with personal development expert and self-made multi-millionaire entrepreneur, Eben Pagan, who was being interviewed by bestselling author Anthony Robbins. Tony asked, "Eben, what is your #1 key to success?" Of course, I was very encouraged when Eben's response was, "Start every morning off with a *personal success ritual.* That is the most important key to success." Then he went on to talk about the importance of morning exercise.

Eben said, "Every morning, you've got to get your heart rate up and get your blood flowing and fill your lungs with oxygen." He continued, "Don't just exercise at the end of the day or at the middle of the day. And even if you do like to exercise at those times, always incorporate at least 10 to 20 minutes of jumping jacks or some sort of aerobic exercise in the morning."

The benefits of morning exercise are too many to ignore. From waking you up and enhancing your mental clarity, to helping you sustain higher levels of energy throughout the day, exercising soon after rising can improve your life in many ways.

Whether you go to the gym, go for a walk or run, throw on a *P90X®* or *Insanity®* DVD, what you do during your period of exercise is up to you, although I'll share some recommendations.

Personally, if I were only allowed to practice one form of exercise for the rest of my life, I would, without a doubt choose yoga. I began practicing yoga shortly after I created *The Miracle Morning*, and have been doing it—and loving it—ever since. It's such a complete form of exercise, as it combines *stretching* with *strength training* with *cardio* with *focused breathing*, and can even be a form of *meditation*.

Meet the One and Only... Dashama

I can't talk about yoga (or exercise for that matter) without talking about my friend Dashama. A few years ago, one of her students introduced me to her work as one of the world's leading yoga instructors. Dashama is the most authentic, spiritual, practical, and all-around most effective yoga teacher I have ever come across. I asked her to share her unique perspective on the benefits of yoga (and I highly recommend getting her free Yoga training videos, available through www.TMMbook.com)

From Dashama: Yoga is a multi-faceted science that has applications for the physical, mental, emotional and spiritual aspects of life. That being said, when Hal asked me to contribute a short introductory to yoga, for this book, I felt it was in perfect alignment with *The Miracle Morning*. I know from personal experience that yoga can help you create miracles in your life. I've experienced it in mine and also witnessed it in countless others whom I have taught around the world.

The important thing to remember is that yoga can take place in many forms. Whether it is sitting in silent meditation, breathing to expand your lung capacity or back bending to open your heart - there are practices that can help every aspect of your life. The key is to learn which techniques to practice when you need a remedy and use it to your advantage to bring yourself into balance.

A well-rounded yoga practice can enhance your life in so many ways. It can heal what is out of harmony and can move stuck or blocked energy through your body, creating space for new fluid movement, blood flow and energy to circulate. I encourage you to listen to your body and try some new sequences as you feel ready. To learn more and see instructional yoga videos, feel free to visit my website at pranashama.com.

Blessings and Love, Dashama

Final Thoughts On Exercise

You know that if you want to maintain good health and increase your energy, you must exercise consistently. That's not news to anybody. But it's too easy to make excuses as to why we don't exercise. Two of the biggest are "I just don't have time" and "I'm just too tired." There is no limit to the excuses that you can think of. The more creative you are the more excuses you can come up with, right?

That's the beauty of incorporating exercise into your *Miracle Morning*; it happens before your day wears you out, before you have a chance to get too tired, before you have an entire day to come up with new excuses for avoiding exercise. *The Miracle Morning* is really a surefire way to avoid all of those excuses, and to make exercise a daily habit. (More on the easy way to implement positive habits into your life, like exercise, in *Chapter 9: From Unbearable To Unstoppable – The Real Secret To Forming Habits That Will Transform Your Life (In 30 Days)* which will enhance your quality of life for years to come.)

Legal disclaimer: Hopefully this goes without saying, but you should consult your doctor or physician before beginning any exercise regimen, especially if you are experiencing any physical pain, discomfort, disabilities, etc. You may need to modify or even refrain from your exercise routine to meet your individual needs.

Life S.A.V.E.**R**.S.

R is for Reading

A person who won't read has no advantage
over one who can't read.
—MARK TWAIN

Reading is to the mind what exercise is to the body and
prayer is to the soul. We become the books we read.
—MATTHEW KELLY

Reading, the fifth practice in the *Life S.A.V.E.R.S.*, is the fast track to transforming any area of your life. It is one of the most immediate methods for acquiring the knowledge, ideas, and strategies you need to achieve *Level 10* success in any area of your life.

The key is to learn from the experts—those who have already done what you want to do. Don't reinvent the wheel. The fastest way to achieve everything you want is to *model* successful people who have already achieved it. With an almost infinite amount of books available on every topic, there are no limits to the knowledge you can gain through daily reading.

I recently heard someone say in a mocking, *I'm too cool for this* tone, "Uh, yeah, I don't read 'self-help' books," as if such books were beneath him. Poor guy. I'm not sure if it's his ego or just lack of awareness, but he's missing out on the unlimited supply of knowledge, boundless growth and life changing ideas he could gain from some of the most brilliant, successful individuals in the world. Who in their right mind would choose *not* to do that?

Whatever you want for your life, there are countless books on how to get it. Want to become wealthy, rich, a multi-millionaire? There are plenty of books written by those who have achieved the pinnacles of financial success, which will teach you how you can do the same. Here are a few of my favorites:

- *Think and Grow Rich* by Napoleon Hill
- *Secrets of the Millionaire Mind* by T. Harv Eker
- *Total Money Makeover* by Dave Ramsey

Want to create an incredible, loving, supportive and romantic relationship? There are probably more books on how to do exactly that than you could read in a decade. Here are a few of my favorites:

- *The Five Love Languages* by Gary D. Chapman
- *The SoulMate Experience* by Jo Dunn
- *The Seven Principles For Making a Marriage Work* by John M. Gottman and Nan Silver

Whether you'd like to transform your relationships, increase your self-confidence, improve your communication or persuasion skills, learn how to become wealthy, or improve any area of your life, head to your local bookstore—or do what I do and head to Amazon.com—and you'll find a plethora of books on any area of your life you want to improve. For those who want to minimize our carbon footprint or save money, I also recommend utilizing your local library or checking out one of my favorite websites, www.paperbackswap.com.

For a complete list of my favorite personal development books—including those that have made the biggest impact on my success and happiness—check out the *Recommended Reading* list located at www.TMMbook.com.

How Much Should You Read?

I recommend making a commitment to read a minimum of 10 pages per day (although five is okay to start with, if you read slowly or don't *yet* enjoy reading). Let's do some math on this for a second: reading 10 pages read per day is not going to break you, but it will *make* you. We're only talking 10-15 minutes of reading, or 15-30 minutes if you read more slowly.

Look at it this way. If you quantify that, reading just 10 pages a day will average 3,650 pages a year, which equates to approximately eighteen 200-page personal development/self-improvement books! Let me ask you, if you read 18 personal development books in the next 12 months, do you think you will be more knowledgeable, capable and confident—a new & improved *you*? Absolutely!

Final Thoughts On Reading

▪ Begin with the end in mind. Before you begin reading each day, ask yourself *why* you are reading that book—what do you want to gain from it—and keep that outcome in mind. Take a moment to do this now by asking yourself what you want to gain from reading *this* book. Are you committed to finishing it? More importantly, are you committed to implementing what you're learning and taking action, by following through with *The Miracle Morning 30-Day Life Transformation Challenge* at the end?

▪ Many *Miracle Morning* practitioners use their Reading time to catch up on their religious texts, such as the Bible, Torah, or any other.

▪ Hopefully you took the advice I gave and you've been underlining, circling, highlighting, folding the corners of pages, and taking notes in the margins of this book. To get the most out of any book I read and make it easy for me to revisit the content again in the future, I underline or circle anything that I may want to re-visit, and make notes in the margins to remind me why I underlined that particular section. (Unless, of course, it's a library book). This process of marking books as I read allows me to come back at anytime and recapture all of the key lessons, ideas, and benefits without needing to read the book again, cover to cover.

I highly recommend *re-reading* good personal development books. Rarely can we read a book once and internalize all of the value from that book. Achieving mastery in any area requires *repetition*—being exposed to certain ideas, strategies, or techniques over and over again, until they become engrained in your subconscious mind. For example, if you wanted to master karate, you wouldn't learn the techniques once and then think, "I've got this?" No, you'd learn the techniques, practice them, then go back to your sensei and learn them again, and repeat the process hundreds of times in order to master a single technique. Mastering techniques to improve your life works the same way.

There is often more value in re-reading a book you already *know* has strategies that can improve your life than there is in reading a new book before you've mastered the strategies in the first. Whenever I'm reading a book that I see can really make an impact on an area of my life, I commit to re-reading that book (or at least re-reading the parts I've underlined, circled and highlighted) as soon as I'm finished going through it the first time. I actually keep a special space on my bookshelf for the books that I want to re-read. I've read books like *Think and Grow Rich* as many as three times, and often refer back to them throughout the year.

Re-reading requires discipline, because it is typically more "fun" to read a book you've never read before. Repetition can be boring or tedious (which is why so few people ever "master" anything), but that's even more reason why we should do it—to develop a higher level of self-discipline. Why not try it out with this book? Commit to re-reading it as soon as you're finished, to deepen your learning and give yourself more time to master *The Miracle Morning*.

S is for Scribing

Whatever it is that you write, putting words on the page
is a form of therapy that doesn't cost a dime.
—DIANA RAAB

Ideas can come from anywhere and at any time. The
problem with making mental notes is that the ink
fades very rapidly.
—ROLF SMITH

Scribing is the final practice in the *Life S.A.V.E.R.S.* and is really just another word for *writing*, but please allow me to keep it real—I needed an 'S' for the end of *Life S.A.V.E.R.S.* because a 'W' wouldn't fit anywhere. Thanks Thesaurus®, I owe you one.

Journaling

My favorite form of Scribing is journaling, which I do for 5-10 minutes during my *Miracle Morning.* By getting your thoughts out of your head and putting them in writing, you gain valuable insights you'd otherwise never see. The Scribing element of your *Miracle Morning* enables you to document your insights, ideas, breakthroughs, realizations, successes, and lessons learned, as well as any areas of opportunity, personal growth, or improvement.

While I had known about the profound benefits of journaling for years—and I had even tried it a few times—I never stuck with it consistently, because it was never part of my daily routine. Usually, I kept a journal by my bed, and when I'd get home late at night, nine times out of ten I would find myself making the excuse that I was too tired to write in it. My journals stayed mostly blank. Even though I already had many mostly blank journals sitting on my bookshelf, every so often I would buy myself a brand new journal—a more expensive one—convincing myself that if I spent a lot of money on it, I would surely write in it. Seems like a decent theory, right? Unfortunately, my little strategy never worked, and for years I just accumulated more and more increasingly expensive, yet equally empty journals.

That was before *The Miracle Morning*. From day one, *The Miracle Morning* gave me the time and structure to write in my journal *every day*, and it quickly became one of my favorite habits. I can tell you now that journaling has become one of the most gratifying and fulfilling practices of my life. Not only do I derive the daily benefits of consciously directing my thoughts and putting them in writing, but even more powerful are those I have gained from reviewing my journals, from cover to cover, afterwards—especially, at the end of the year. It is hard to put into words how overwhelmingly constructive the experience of going back and reviewing your journals can be, but I'll do my best.

My First Journal Re-view

On December 31st, after my first year doing *The Miracle Morning* and writing in my journal, I began reading the first page I had written that year. Day by day, I started to review and *relive* my entire year. I was able to revisit my mindset from each day, and gain a new perspective as to how much I had grown throughout the year. I reexamined my actions, activities, and progress, giving me a new appreciation for how much I had accomplished during the past 12 months. Most importantly, I recaptured the lessons I had learned, many of which I had forgotten over the course of the year.

Gratitude 2.0 – I also experienced a much deeper quality of gratitude—in a way that I had never experienced before—on two different levels, simultaneously. It was what I now refer to as my first *Back to the Future* moment. Try to follow me here (and feel free to picture me as Marty McFly stepping out of a 1985 DeLorean). As I read through my journal, my current self (which was also the *future* self of who I was at the time I wrote those journal entries) was now looking back at all of the people, experiences, lessons, and accomplishments that I took note of being grateful for throughout the year. As I was in that moment reliving the gratitude that I felt in the past, I was simultaneously feeling grateful in the present moment for how far I had come since that time in my life. It was a remarkable experience, and a bit surreal.

Accelerated Growth – Then, I began to tap into the highest point of value I would gain from reviewing my journals. I pulled out a sheet of blank paper, drew a line down the middle, and wrote two headings at the top: *Lessons Learned* and *New Commitments*. As I read through my hundreds of my journal entries, I found myself recapturing dozens of valuable lessons.

This process of recapturing *Lessons Learned* and making *New Commitments* to implement those lessons aided my personal growth and development more than almost anything else.

While there are many worthwhile benefits of keeping a daily journal, a few of which I've just described, here are a few more of my favorites:

- **Gain Clarity** – The process of writing something down forces us to think through it enough to understand it. Journaling will give you more clarity, allow you to brainstorm, and help you work through problems.

- **Capture Ideas** – Journaling helps you not only expand your ideas, but also prevents you from losing the important ideas that you may want to act on in the future.

- **Review Lessons** – It enables you to review all of the lessons you've learned.

- **Acknowledge Your Progress** – It's wonderful to go back and re-read your journal entries from a year ago and see how much progress you've made. It's one of the most empowering, confidence-inspiring and enjoyable experiences. It can't really be duplicated any other way.

Gap-Focus: Is It Hurting or Helping You?

In the opening pages of this chapter, we talked about using the *Life S.A.V.E.R.S.* to close your "Potential Gap." Human beings are conditioned to have what I call *gap-focus*. We tend to focus on the gaps between where we are in life and where we want to be, between what we've accomplished and what we could have or want to accomplish, and the gap between who we are and our idealistic vision of the person we believe we should be.

The problem with this is that constant gap-focus can be detrimental to our confidence and self-image, causing us to feel like we don't have enough, haven't accomplished enough, and that we're simply not good enough, or at least, not as good as we should be.

High achievers are typically the worst at this, constantly overlooking or minimizing their accomplishments, beating themselves up over every mistake and imperfection, and never feeling like anything they do is quite good enough.

The irony is that gap-focus is a big part of the reason that high achievers *are* high achievers. Their insatiable desire to close the gap is what fuels their pursuit of excellence and constantly drives them to achieve. Gap-focus can be healthy and productive if it comes from a positive, proactive, "I'm committed to and excited about fulfilling my potential" perspective, without any feelings of lack. Unfortunately, it rarely does. The average person, even the average high achiever, tends to focus negatively on their gaps.

The *highest* achievers—those who are balanced and focused on achieving *Level 10* success in nearly every area of their lives—are exceedingly grateful for what they have, regularly acknowledge themselves for what they've accomplished, and are always at peace with where they are in their lives. It's the dueling idea that *I am doing the best that I can in this moment, and at the same time, I can and will do better.* This balanced self-assessment prevents that feeling of lack—of not being, having, doing enough—while still allowing them to constantly strive to close their potential gap in each area.

Typically, when a day, week, month, or year ends, and we're in Gap-focus mode, it's almost impossible to maintain an accurate assessment of ourselves and our progress. For example, if you had 10 things on your to-do list for the day—even if you completed six of them—your gap-focus causes you to feel you didn't get everything done that you wanted to do.

The majority of people do dozens, even hundreds, of things *right* during the day, and a few things wrong. Guess which things people remember and replay in their minds over and over again? Doesn't it make more sense to focus on the 100 things you did right? It sure is more enjoyable.

What does this have to do with writing in a journal? Writing in a journal each day, with a *structured*, strategic process (more on that in a minute) allows you to direct your focus to what you did accomplish, what you're grateful for, and what you're committed to doing better tomorrow. Thus, you more deeply enjoy your journey each day, feel good about any forward progress you made, and use a heightened level of clarity to accelerate your results.

Write What Comes Naturally

There are infinite aspects of your life that you can write about in your *Miracle Morning* Journal about. You can write about your goals, dreams, and plans to achieve them. You can document what you're grateful for and what it means to you to be grateful for those things. You can record the day's events, lessons learned, and anything else that you feel you need to focus on in your life.

My journaling method ranges from being a very specific, structured process—*listing what I'm grateful for, acknowledging my accomplishments, clarifying what areas I want to improve on, and planning which specific actions I'm committed to taking to improve*—to being pretty traditional, just a dated entry with a synopsis of my day. I find both to be very valuable, and it's nice to mix it up.

To share a free sample of *The Miracle Morning Journal* with your friends, family, and co-workers, simply send them to www.TMMbook.com.

Customizing The Life S.A.V.E.R.S.

In *Chapter 8: Customizing The Miracle Morning To Fit Your Lifestyle*, you'll learn how you can personalize and customize nearly every aspect of your *Miracle Morning* to fit your lifestyle. For now, I want to share a few ideas specifically toward customizing the *Life S.A.V.E.R.S.* based on your schedule and preferences. Your current morning routine might only allow you to fit in a 20 or 30-minute *Miracle Morning*, or you might choose to do a longer version on the weekends.

Here is an example of a fairly common, 60-minute *Miracle Morning* schedule, using the *Life S.A.V.E.R.S.*

The Miracle Morning (60-min.) Sample Schedule:

— Using The Life S.A.V.E.R.S. —

√ **S**ilence (5 minutes)

√ **A**ffirmations (5 minutes)

√ **V**isualization (5 minutes)

√ **E**xercise (20 minutes)

√ **R**eading (20 minutes)

√ **S**cribing (5 minutes)

Total Time: 60 minutes

The sequence in which you do the *Life S.A.V.E.R.S.* can also be customized to your preferences. Some people prefer to do their *Exercise* first, as a way to increase their blood flow and wake themselves up. However, you might prefer to do *Exercise* as your last activity in the *Life S.A.V.E.R.S.* so you're not sweaty during your *Miracle Morning.* Personally, I prefer to start with a period of peaceful, purposeful *Silence*—so that I can wake up slowly, clear my mind, and focus my energy and intentions. I save *Exercise* for my last activity, that way I can jump directly into the shower and proceed with the rest of my day. However, this is *your Miracle Morning*—not mine—so feel free to experiment with different sequences and see which you like best.

Final Thoughts On The Life S.A.V.E.R.S.

Everything is difficult before it's easy. Every new experience is uncomfortable before it's comfortable. The more you practice the *Life S.A.V.E.R.S.* the more natural and normal each of them will feel. Remember that my first time meditating was almost my last, as my mind raced like a Ferrari and my thoughts bounced around uncontrollably like the silver sphere in a pinball machine. Now, I love meditation, and while I'm no *master*, I'd say I'm decent at it. Similarly, my first time doing yoga, I felt like a fish out of water. I wasn't flexible, couldn't do the poses correctly, and felt awkward and uncomfortable.

Now, yoga is my favorite form of exercise, and I am so grateful that I stuck with it.

I invite you to begin practicing the Life *S.A.V.E.R.S.* now, so you can become familiar and comfortable with each of them, and get a jump-start before you begin *The Miracle Morning 30-Day Life Transformation Challenge* in Chapter 10. If your biggest concern is still *finding time*, don't worry, I've got you covered. In the next chapter, you're going to learn how to do the entire Miracle Morning— receiving the full benefits from all six of the *Life S.A.V.E.R.S.*—in only 6 minutes a day.

The 6-Minute Miracle Morning
(For The Busy People)

On the one hand, we all want to be happy. On the other hand,
we all know the things that make us happy. But we don't do those
things. Why? Simple. We are too busy. Too busy doing what?
Too busy trying to be happy.
—MATTHEW KELLY

I don't have time to wake up early.
—UNKNOWN

Ohhh, you're busy? Weird. I thought it was just me.

Probably the most common question—or concern—I get about *The Miracle Morning* is regarding *how long it needs to be*. When I first had the breakthrough realization about how our levels of success (and fulfilling our potential) in every area of life are being limited by our insufficient (or non-existent) level of personal development, my biggest challenge was *finding time* to act on this realization.

As I've developed and shared *The Miracle Morning* over the years, I've been very aware of the need to make it scalable so that even the busiest among us can make time for our *Miracle Morning*. I developed *The 6-minute Miracle Morning* for those days when you're extra busy and pressed for time, as well as for those of you who are so overwhelmed with your life situation right now that just thinking about adding *one more thing* stresses you out.

I think we can all agree that investing a minimum of six minutes into becoming the person we need to be to create the levels of success and happiness we truly want in our lives is not only reasonable, it's an

45

absolute must, even when we're pressed for time. I think you will be pleasantly surprised in the next few minutes as you read and realize how *powerful* (and life-changing) these six minutes can be!

Imagine if the first six minutes of every morning began like this…

Minute One…

Envision yourself waking up peacefully in the morning, with a big yawn, a stretch, and a smile on your face. Instead of rushing carelessly into your hectic day—stressed and overwhelmed—you spend the first minute sitting quietly, in purposeful *Silence*. You sit, very calm, very peaceful, and breathe deeply, slowly. Maybe you say a prayer of gratitude to appreciate the moment, or pray for guidance on your journey. Maybe you decide to try your first minute of meditation. As you sit in silence, you're totally present in the now, in the moment. You calm your mind, relax your body, and allow all of your stress to melt away. You develop a deeper sense of peace, purpose, and direction…

Minute Two…

You pull out your daily *Affirmations*—the ones that remind you of your unlimited potential and your most important priorities—and you read them out loud from top to bottom. As you focus on what's most important to you, your level of internal motivation increases. Reading over the reminders of how capable you *really* are gives you a feeling of confidence. Looking over what you're committed to, what your purpose is, and what your goals are re-energizes you to take the actions necessary to *live* the life you truly want, deserve, and now *know* is possible for you…

Minute Three…

You close your eyes, or you look at your vision board, and you visualize. Your *Visualization* could include what it will look and feel like when you reach your goals. You visualize the day going perfectly, see yourself enjoying your work, smiling and laughing with your family or your significant other, and easily accomplishing all that you intend to accomplish for that day. You see what it will look like, you feel what it will feel like, and you experience the joy of what you will create…

Minute Four...

You take one minute to write down some of the things that you're grateful for, what you're proud of, and the results you're committed to creating for that day. In doing so, you create for yourself an empowered, inspired, and confident state of mind...

Minute Five...

Then, you grab your self-help book and invest one miraculous minute reading a page or two. You learn a new idea, something you can incorporate into your day which will improve your results at work or in your relationships. You discover something new that you can use to think and feel better—to *live* better...

Minute Six...

Finally, you stand up and spend the last minute moving your body for 60 seconds. Maybe you run in place, maybe you do a minute of jumping-jacks. Maybe you do push-ups or sit-ups. The point is that you're getting your heart rate up, generating energy and increasing your ability to be alert and focused.

How would you feel if that's how you utilized the first 6-minutes of each day? How would the quality of your day—your life—improve?

I don't suggest you limit your *Miracle Morning* to only six minutes every day, but as I said, on those days when you're pressed for time, *The 6-minute Miracle Morning* provides a powerful strategy for accelerating your personal development.

→**Top Weekly Goals/Commitments** – The top 3-5 goals that I am 100% committed to achieving this week are:

_____
_____
_____
_____
_____
_____

The **Life** S.A.V.E.R.S. Mark each practice that you complete each day.

⇒ Silence............................ ☐ M ☐ T ☐ W ☐ Th ☐ F ☐ S ☐ S
⇒ Affirmations................ ☐ M ☐ T ☐ W ☐ Th ☐ F ☐ S ☐ S
⇒ Visualization.............. ☐ M ☐ T ☐ W ☐ Th ☐ F ☐ S ☐ S
⇒ Exercise........................ ☐ M ☐ T ☐ W ☐ Th ☐ F ☐ S ☐ S
⇒ Reading......................... ☐ M ☐ T ☐ W ☐ Th ☐ F ☐ S ☐ S
⇒ Scribing........................ ☐ M ☐ T ☐ W ☐ Th ☐ F ☐ S ☐ S

Monday [____] – I am ready and committed to make this my best year yet

_____
_____
_____
_____
_____
_____

Tuesday [____] – I love the life I have while I create the life of my dreams

_____
_____
_____
_____
_____
_____

Wednesday [____] – I dedicate time to *The Miracle Morning* every day so that I can become the person I need to be to create the life I truly want & deserve

_____
_____
_____
_____
_____
_____

Thursday [____] – I am grateful for all that I have, accepting of all that I don't, and I actively create all that I want

_____

_____

_____

_____

_____

Friday [____] – Everyone has value to share, so I learn something from everyone

_____

_____

_____

_____

_____

Saturday [____] – I am giving up the need to be perfect for the opportunity to be authentic

_____

_____

_____

_____

_____

Sunday [____] – I learn from my mistakes and improve every week

_____

_____

_____

_____

_____

[Weekly Review] What were my accomplishments and disappointments? What commitments will I make NOW to ensure that I improve next week?

_____

_____

_____

_____

_____

→**Top Weekly Goals/Commitments** – The top 3-5 goals that I am 100% committed to achieving this week are:

_____
_____
_____
_____
_____

The Life S.A.V.E.R.S. Mark each practice that you complete each day.

⇒   Silence............................. ☐ M ☐ T ☐ W ☐ Th ☐ F ☐ S ☐ S
⇒   Affirmations............... ☐ M ☐ T ☐ W ☐ Th ☐ F ☐ S ☐ S
⇒   Visualization............... ☐ M ☐ T ☐ W ☐ Th ☐ F ☐ S ☐ S
⇒   Exercise......................... ☐ M ☐ T ☐ W ☐ Th ☐ F ☐ S ☐ S
⇒   Reading........................... ☐ M ☐ T ☐ W ☐ Th ☐ F ☐ S ☐ S
⇒   Scribing........................... ☐ M ☐ T ☐ W ☐ Th ☐ F ☐ S ☐ S

Monday [_____] – I am exactly where I'm supposed to be to learn what I need to learn, in order to become the person I must be to create the life I want

_____
_____
_____
_____
_____

Tuesday [_____] – Worry is a misuse of the imagination, so I imagine greatness

_____
_____
_____
_____

Wednesday [_____] – I am capable of achieving anything I fully commit to

_____
_____
_____
_____
_____

Thursday [____] – I strive to make *every day* the best day of my life, because there is simply no good reason not to

_____

_____

_____

_____

_____

Friday [____] – No matter how it started, I'm going to finish the week strong

_____

_____

_____

_____

_____

Saturday [____] – I'm grateful for the gift of weekends

_____

_____

_____

_____

_____

Sunday [____] – I'm committed to doing what is necessary to make the coming week even better than the last

_____

_____

_____

_____

_____

[Weekly Review] What were my accomplishments and disappointments? What commitments will I make NOW to ensure that I improve next week?

_____

_____

_____

_____

_____

➜**Top Weekly Goals/Commitments** – The top 3-5 goals that I am 100% committed to achieving this week are:

_____

_____

_____

_____

_____

The Life S.A.V.E.R.S. Mark each practice that you complete each day.

⇒ Silence................................ ☐ M ☐ T ☐ W ☐ Th ☐ F ☐ S ☐ S
⇒ Affirmations................... ☐ M ☐ T ☐ W ☐ Th ☐ F ☐ S ☐ S
⇒ Visualization................. ☐ M ☐ T ☐ W ☐ Th ☐ F ☐ S ☐ S
⇒ Exercise.......................... ☐ M ☐ T ☐ W ☐ Th ☐ F ☐ S ☐ S
⇒ Reading............................ ☐ M ☐ T ☐ W ☐ Th ☐ F ☐ S ☐ S
⇒ Scribing........................... ☐ M ☐ T ☐ W ☐ Th ☐ F ☐ S ☐ S

Monday [____] – I love the life I have, because it's the only life I have

_____

_____

_____

_____

_____

Tuesday [____] – I accept and am at peace with all things that I can't change

_____

_____

_____

_____

_____

Wednesday [____] – I change everything that I have the power to change

_____

_____

_____

_____

_____

Thursday [____] – Although others settle for mediocrity, I will not

_____
_____
_____
_____
_____
_____

Friday [____] – I am just as deserving and capable of success as anyone else

_____
_____
_____
_____
_____
_____

Saturday [____] – I am destined for greatness—to be precisely as great as I choose to be

_____
_____
_____
_____
_____
_____

Sunday [____] – My challenges are an opportunity for me to learn & grow

_____
_____
_____
_____
_____
_____

[Weekly Review] What were my accomplishments and disappointments? What commitments will I make NOW to ensure that I improve next week?

_____
_____
_____
_____
_____
_____

→**Top Weekly Goals/Commitments** – The top 3-5 goals that I am 100% committed to achieving this week are:

_____

_____

_____

_____

_____

The Life S.A.V.E.R.S. Mark each practice that you complete each day.

⇒ Silence............................ ☐ M ☐ T ☐ W ☐ Th ☐ F ☐ S ☐ S
⇒ Affirmations............... ☐ M ☐ T ☐ W ☐ Th ☐ F ☐ S ☐ S
⇒ Visualization.............. ☐ M ☐ T ☐ W ☐ Th ☐ F ☐ S ☐ S
⇒ Exercise......................... ☐ M ☐ T ☐ W ☐ Th ☐ F ☐ S ☐ S
⇒ Reading.......................... ☐ M ☐ T ☐ W ☐ Th ☐ F ☐ S ☐ S
⇒ Scribing......................... ☐ M ☐ T ☐ W ☐ Th ☐ F ☐ S ☐ S

Monday [____] – I know that TODAY is the most important day of my life, because it is what I do and who I become today that will determine my future

_____

_____

_____

_____

_____

Tuesday [____] – I appreciate and find joy in every moment

_____

_____

_____

_____

_____

Wednesday [____] – I wake up every day *on purpose* to create my life

_____

_____

_____

_____

_____

Thursday [____] – I know that where I am is a result of who I *was*, but where I go depends entirely on whom I choose to be from this day forward

_____

_____

_____

_____

_____

Friday [____] – I love myself and others, unconditionally

_____

_____

_____

_____

_____

Saturday [____] – Everything happens for a reason, but it is my responsibility to choose the most empowering reasons for the events & challenges of my life

_____

_____

_____

_____

_____

Sunday [____] – I have the ability to change or create anything for my life

_____

_____

_____

_____

_____

[Weekly Review] What were my accomplishments and disappointments? What commitments will I make NOW to ensure that I improve next week?

_____

_____

_____

_____

_____

→**Top Weekly Goals/Commitments** – The top 3-5 goals that I am 100% committed to achieving this week are:

_____

_____

_____

_____

_____

The Life S.A.V.E.R.S. Mark each practice that you complete each day.

		M	T	W	Th	F	S	S
⇒	Silence................................	☐	☐	☐	☐	☐	☐	☐
⇒	Affirmations..................	☐	☐	☐	☐	☐	☐	☐
⇒	Visualization.................	☐	☐	☐	☐	☐	☐	☐
⇒	Exercise.........................	☐	☐	☐	☐	☐	☐	☐
⇒	Reading..........................	☐	☐	☐	☐	☐	☐	☐
⇒	Scribing..........................	☐	☐	☐	☐	☐	☐	☐

Monday [____] – I know that who I'm becoming is far more important that what I'm doing, but it is what I am doing that is determining who I become

_____

_____

_____

_____

_____

Tuesday [____] – I see the best in myself and others

_____

_____

_____

_____

Wednesday [____] – I talk positively to myself to inspire self-confidence

_____

_____

_____

_____

_____

Thursday [____] – I regularly invest time to dream of my compelling future

_____

_____

_____

_____

_____

Friday [____] – I take actions daily to create progress towards my highest goals & dreams, because I know anything can be achieved one day at a time

_____

_____

_____

_____

_____

Saturday [____] – I accept responsibility for EVERY aspect of my life, so that I am the only person with the power to affect my life

_____

_____

_____

_____

_____

Sunday [____] – I believe in my ability to make the impossible possible

_____

_____

_____

_____

_____

[Weekly Review] What were my accomplishments and disappointments? What commitments will I make NOW to ensure that I improve next week?

_____

_____

_____

_____

_____

_____

→Top Weekly Goals/Commitments – The top 3-5 goals that I am 100% committed to achieving this week are:

_____
_____
_____
_____
_____

The **Life S.A.V.E.R.S.** Mark each practice that you complete each day.

⇒ Silence.............................. ☐ M ☐ T ☐ W ☐ Th ☐ F ☐ S ☐ S
⇒ Affirmations............... ☐ M ☐ T ☐ W ☐ Th ☐ F ☐ S ☐ S
⇒ Visualization................ ☐ M ☐ T ☐ W ☐ Th ☐ F ☐ S ☐ S
⇒ Exercise.......................... ☐ M ☐ T ☐ W ☐ Th ☐ F ☐ S ☐ S
⇒ Reading........................... ☐ M ☐ T ☐ W ☐ Th ☐ F ☐ S ☐ S
⇒ Scribing........................... ☐ M ☐ T ☐ W ☐ Th ☐ F ☐ S ☐ S

Monday [____] – I believe that the more value I add to the lives of others, the more valuable I become to the people who most significantly impact my life

_____
_____
_____
_____
_____

Tuesday [____] – The more I give I give to others, the more I receive

_____
_____
_____
_____
_____

Wednesday [____] – I am grateful for my everything I have today

_____
_____
_____
_____
_____

Thursday [____] – I will grow and develop myself to be bigger than any problem that will ever come my way

_____
_____
_____
_____
_____
_____

Friday [____] – I learn from every situation, good or bad

_____
_____
_____
_____
_____
_____

Saturday [____] – I know that we become like the people we spend the most time with, so I choose to seek out and spend time with winners

_____
_____
_____
_____
_____
_____

Sunday [____] – I will do something today that serves someone else

_____
_____
_____
_____
_____
_____

[Weekly Review] What were my accomplishments and disappointments? What commitments will I make NOW to ensure that I improve next week?

_____
_____
_____
_____
_____
_____

→**Top Weekly Goals/Commitments** – The top 3-5 goals that I am 100% committed to achieving this week are:

_____

_____

_____

_____

_____

_____

The Life S.A.V.E.R.S. Mark each practice that you complete each day.

⇒ Silence............................ ☐ M ☐ T ☐ W ☐ Th ☐ F ☐ S ☐ S
⇒ Affirmations............... ☐ M ☐ T ☐ W ☐ Th ☐ F ☐ S ☐ S
⇒ Visualization.............. ☐ M ☐ T ☐ W ☐ Th ☐ F ☐ S ☐ S
⇒ Exercise......................... ☐ M ☐ T ☐ W ☐ Th ☐ F ☐ S ☐ S
⇒ Reading.......................... ☐ M ☐ T ☐ W ☐ Th ☐ F ☐ S ☐ S
⇒ Scribing......................... ☐ M ☐ T ☐ W ☐ Th ☐ F ☐ S ☐ S

Monday [_____] – I win because I am persistent

_____

_____

_____

_____

_____

Tuesday [_____] – I avoid complaining because it only hurts me and those around me

_____

_____

_____

_____

_____

Wednesday [_____] – I set goals and make plans to reach them

_____

_____

_____

_____

_____

Thursday [____] – I will grow as a person and give it everything I have until the last possible moment, regardless of the results

_____

_____

_____

_____

_____

_____

Friday [____] – I will improve myself in all areas of my life

_____

_____

_____

_____

_____

_____

Saturday [____] – I will consult winners for winning ideas

_____

_____

_____

_____

_____

_____

Sunday [____] – I will grow and move beyond my present circumstances

_____

_____

_____

_____

_____

_____

[Weekly Review] What were my accomplishments and disappointments? What commitments will I make NOW to ensure that I improve next week?

_____

_____

_____

_____

_____

_____

➔Top Weekly Goals/Commitments – The top 3-5 goals that I am 100% committed to achieving this week are:

_____
_____
_____
_____
_____

The Life S.A.V.E.R.S. Mark each practice that you complete each day.

⇒ Silence............................ ☐ M ☐ T ☐ W ☐ Th ☐ F ☐ S ☐ S
⇒ Affirmations.............. ☐ M ☐ T ☐ W ☐ Th ☐ F ☐ S ☐ S
⇒ Visualization............... ☐ M ☐ T ☐ W ☐ Th ☐ F ☐ S ☐ S
⇒ Exercise......................... ☐ M ☐ T ☐ W ☐ Th ☐ F ☐ S ☐ S
⇒ Reading.......................... ☐ M ☐ T ☐ W ☐ Th ☐ F ☐ S ☐ S
⇒ Scribing......................... ☐ M ☐ T ☐ W ☐ Th ☐ F ☐ S ☐ S

Monday [____] – I will do something selfless today or this week that serves someone else without expecting anything in return

_____
_____
_____
_____
_____

Tuesday [____] – I will be more grateful and less worried

_____
_____
_____
_____

Wednesday [____] – I enjoy whatever I am doing

_____
_____
_____
_____
_____

Thursday [____] – I will not let fears, insecurities, and limiting beliefs of others limit what's possible for me

_____
_____
_____
_____
_____
_____

Friday [____] – I will earn the right to be successful

_____
_____
_____
_____
_____
_____

Saturday [____] – I will be grateful for my challenges, disappointments, and inconveniences because it is all a part of becoming who I want to be

_____
_____
_____
_____
_____
_____

Sunday [____] – I will challenge myself as well as others

_____
_____
_____
_____
_____
_____

[Weekly Review] What were my accomplishments and disappointments? What commitments will I make NOW to ensure that I improve next week?

_____
_____
_____
_____
_____
_____

→Top Weekly Goals/Commitments – The top 3-5 goals that I am 100% committed to achieving this week are:

_____

_____

_____

_____

_____

The Life S.A.V.E.R.S. Mark each practice that you complete each day.

⇒ Silence............................ ☐ M ☐ T ☐ W ☐ Th ☐ F ☐ S ☐ S
⇒ Affirmations................ ☐ M ☐ T ☐ W ☐ Th ☐ F ☐ S ☐ S
⇒ Visualization................ ☐ M ☐ T ☐ W ☐ Th ☐ F ☐ S ☐ S
⇒ Exercise.......................... ☐ M ☐ T ☐ W ☐ Th ☐ F ☐ S ☐ S
⇒ Reading.......................... ☐ M ☐ T ☐ W ☐ Th ☐ F ☐ S ☐ S
⇒ Scribing.......................... ☐ M ☐ T ☐ W ☐ Th ☐ F ☐ S ☐ S

Monday [_____] – It's never too late for me to do the right thing, right now

_____

_____

_____

_____

_____

Tuesday [_____] – I will not lose sight of the miracle that I am living each day

_____

_____

_____

_____

Wednesday [_____] – I will be honest with myself and others

_____

_____

_____

_____

_____

Thursday [_____] – I will meet all challenges with determination

_____
_____
_____
_____
_____

Friday [_____] – I will focus on the positive aspects of my life that make me feel good, rather than the negative aspects that make me feel discouraged

_____
_____
_____
_____
_____

Saturday [_____] – I will maintain faith, stay committed, follow through, and keep moving forward until I make it to my highest goals and dreams

_____
_____
_____
_____
_____

Sunday [_____] – My enthusiasm will add energy and pleasure to my life

_____
_____
_____
_____
_____

[Weekly Review] What were my accomplishments and disappointments? What commitments will I make NOW to ensure that I improve next week?

_____
_____
_____
_____
_____

➔**Top Weekly Goals/Commitments** – The top 3-5 goals that I am 100% committed to achieving this week are:

_____
_____
_____
_____
_____

The Life S.A.V.E.R.S. Mark each practice that you complete each day.
⇒ Silence.............................. ☐ M ☐ T ☐ W ☐ Th ☐ F ☐ S ☐ S
⇒ Affirmations............... ☐ M ☐ T ☐ W ☐ Th ☐ F ☐ S ☐ S
⇒ Visualization................ ☐ M ☐ T ☐ W ☐ Th ☐ F ☐ S ☐ S
⇒ Exercise......................... ☐ M ☐ T ☐ W ☐ Th ☐ F ☐ S ☐ S
⇒ Reading.......................... ☐ M ☐ T ☐ W ☐ Th ☐ F ☐ S ☐ S
⇒ Scribing.......................... ☐ M ☐ T ☐ W ☐ Th ☐ F ☐ S ☐ S

Monday [_____] – Today and every day, I will choose do what's right, not what's easy

_____
_____
_____
_____
_____

Tuesday [_____] – I will learn something from every person I meet

_____
_____
_____
_____
_____

Wednesday [_____] – I will meet all challenges with determination

_____
_____
_____
_____
_____

Thursday [_____] – I am just as worthy, and capable of achieving the highest levels of success as any other person on earth

_____
_____
_____
_____
_____

Friday [_____] – I will refuse to accept defeat

_____
_____
_____
_____
_____

Saturday [_____] – I will choose to be better than I've been in the past

_____
_____
_____
_____
_____

Sunday [_____] – I will hold other people to higher standards to bring out the best in them

_____
_____
_____
_____
_____

[Weekly Review] What were my accomplishments and disappointments? What commitments will I make NOW to ensure that I improve next week?

_____
_____
_____
_____
_____

➔**Top Weekly Goals/Commitments** – The top 3-5 goals that I am 100% committed to achieving this week are:

_____

_____

_____

_____

_____

The Life S.A.V.E.R.S. Mark each practice that you complete each day.							
⇒ Silence..........................	☐ M	☐ T	☐ W	☐ Th	☐ F	☐ S	☐ S
⇒ Affirmations...............	☐ M	☐ T	☐ W	☐ Th	☐ F	☐ S	☐ S
⇒ Visualization..............	☐ M	☐ T	☐ W	☐ Th	☐ F	☐ S	☐ S
⇒ Exercise......................	☐ M	☐ T	☐ W	☐ Th	☐ F	☐ S	☐ S
⇒ Reading.......................	☐ M	☐ T	☐ W	☐ Th	☐ F	☐ S	☐ S
⇒ Scribing......................	☐ M	☐ T	☐ W	☐ Th	☐ F	☐ S	☐ S

Monday [____] – I will take action, even when I don't feel like it

_____

_____

_____

_____

_____

Tuesday [____] – I will genuinely care about others' success

_____

_____

_____

_____

Wednesday [____] – I will replace my judgments with empathy, upgrade my complaining to gratitude, and trade in my fear for love

_____

_____

_____

_____

Thursday [____] – I will picture myself as already achieving the levels of success I want, and then I will live today in alignment with that vision

_____

_____

_____

_____

_____

_____

Friday [____] – I will allow myself to think BIGGER and act BOLDER

_____

_____

_____

_____

_____

Saturday [____] – By finding ways to help others experience happiness, I will experience it too

_____

_____

_____

_____

_____

Sunday [____] – I will live inspired and fulfilled every day

_____

_____

_____

_____

_____

[Weekly Review] What were my accomplishments and disappointments? What commitments will I make NOW to ensure that I improve next week?

_____

_____

_____

_____

_____

➔**Top Weekly Goals/Commitments** – The top 3-5 goals that I am 100% committed to achieving this week are:

_____

_____

_____

_____

_____

_____

The Life S.A.V.E.R.S. Mark each practice that you complete each day.

		M	T	W	Th	F	S	S
⇒	Silence..............................	☐	☐	☐	☐	☐	☐	☐
⇒	Affirmations.................	☐	☐	☐	☐	☐	☐	☐
⇒	Visualization................	☐	☐	☐	☐	☐	☐	☐
⇒	Exercise..........................	☐	☐	☐	☐	☐	☐	☐
⇒	Reading...........................	☐	☐	☐	☐	☐	☐	☐
⇒	Scribing..........................	☐	☐	☐	☐	☐	☐	☐

Monday [____] – I will be open to new experiences

_____

_____

_____

_____

_____

_____

Tuesday [____] – I will feel the fear and do it anyway because doing something I haven't done before is always worth it

_____

_____

_____

_____

_____

_____

Wednesday [____] – I will change the impossible to possible

_____

_____

_____

_____

_____

_____

Thursday [____] – I am as intelligent, capable, and deserving of extraordinary success as any other person

_____

_____

_____

_____

_____

_____

Friday [____] – I will live my life by choice, not by chance

_____

_____

_____

_____

_____

_____

Saturday [____] – I will uplift my thoughts to uplift my life

_____

_____

_____

_____

_____

_____

Sunday [____] – I will be grateful, rather than complain, because gratitude will serve me better

_____

_____

_____

_____

_____

_____

[Weekly Review] What were my accomplishments and disappointments? What commitments will I make NOW to ensure that I improve next week?

_____

_____

_____

_____

_____

→**Top Weekly Goals/Commitments** – The top 3-5 goals that I am 100% committed to achieving this week are:

_____

_____

_____

_____

_____

The **Life S.A.V.E.R.S.** Mark each practice that you complete each day.

		M	T	W	Th	F	S	S
⇒	Silence............................	☐	☐	☐	☐	☐	☐	☐
⇒	Affirmations...............	☐	☐	☐	☐	☐	☐	☐
⇒	Visualization...............	☐	☐	☐	☐	☐	☐	☐
⇒	Exercise.........................	☐	☐	☐	☐	☐	☐	☐
⇒	Reading..........................	☐	☐	☐	☐	☐	☐	☐
⇒	Scribing.........................	☐	☐	☐	☐	☐	☐	☐

Monday [____] – I will appreciate the ones I love because they are all that I really need

_____

_____

_____

_____

_____

Tuesday [____] – I will make my own destiny

_____

_____

_____

_____

_____

Wednesday [____] – I think, act, and feel like the winner I am

_____

_____

_____

_____

_____

Thursday [____] – I will accept what already is—the past that I cannot change—so there is space to create what can be

_____

_____

_____

_____

_____

Friday [____] – My happiness will multiply as I divide it with others

_____

_____

_____

_____

_____

Saturday [____] – When it doubt, I will always choose love and gratitude

_____

_____

_____

_____

_____

Sunday [____] – I will make my positive thoughts grow stronger with constant repetition

_____

_____

_____

_____

_____

[Weekly Review] What were my accomplishments and disappointments? What commitments will I make NOW to ensure that I improve next week?

_____

_____

_____

_____

_____

➜Top Weekly Goals/Commitments – The top 3-5 goals that I am 100% committed to achieving this week are:

_____

_____

_____

_____

_____

The Life S.A.V.E.R.S. Mark each practice that you complete each day.

⇒ Silence............................ ☐ M ☐ T ☐ W ☐ Th ☐ F ☐ S ☐ S
⇒ Affirmations............... ☐ M ☐ T ☐ W ☐ Th ☐ F ☐ S ☐ S
⇒ Visualization............... ☐ M ☐ T ☐ W ☐ Th ☐ F ☐ S ☐ S
⇒ Exercise......................... ☐ M ☐ T ☐ W ☐ Th ☐ F ☐ S ☐ S
⇒ Reading........................... ☐ M ☐ T ☐ W ☐ Th ☐ F ☐ S ☐ S
⇒ Scribing.......................... ☐ M ☐ T ☐ W ☐ Th ☐ F ☐ S ☐ S

Monday [____] – I will wake up early every day so that while others sleep, I can dream of what's to come

_____

_____

_____

_____

_____

_____

Tuesday [____] – I will focus on what I want to achieve

_____

_____

_____

_____

_____

Wednesday [____] – I will look for new worlds to conquer

_____

_____

_____

_____

_____

_____

Thursday [____] – I will write my ideas down so that it sinks into my subconscious

_____

_____

_____

_____

_____

Friday [____] – I will succeed at the highest level when I love my family, love my work, and am unconditionally grateful for every moment of my life

_____

_____

_____

_____

_____

Saturday [____] – I will focus on what I want to achieve

_____

_____

_____

_____

_____

Sunday [____] – Each day will bring me opportunities to achieve

_____

_____

_____

_____

_____

[Weekly Review] What were my accomplishments and disappointments? What commitments will I make NOW to ensure that I improve next week?

_____

_____

_____

_____

_____

→**Top Weekly Goals/Commitments** – The top 3-5 goals that I am 100% committed to achieving this week are:

_____

_____

_____

_____

_____

The Life S.A.V.E.R.S. Mark each practice that you complete each day.

⇒ Silence............................ ☐ M ☐ T ☐ W ☐ Th ☐ F ☐ S ☐ S
⇒ Affirmations............... ☐ M ☐ T ☐ W ☐ Th ☐ F ☐ S ☐ S
⇒ Visualization.............. ☐ M ☐ T ☐ W ☐ Th ☐ F ☐ S ☐ S
⇒ Exercise......................... ☐ M ☐ T ☐ W ☐ Th ☐ F ☐ S ☐ S
⇒ Reading.......................... ☐ M ☐ T ☐ W ☐ Th ☐ F ☐ S ☐ S
⇒ Scribing......................... ☐ M ☐ T ☐ W ☐ Th ☐ F ☐ S ☐ S

Monday [____] – Let today be your day

_____

_____

_____

_____

_____

Tuesday [____] – Instead of stressing I will believe that life is a blessing

_____

_____

_____

_____

_____

Wednesday – I will let today be the day

_____

_____

_____

_____

_____

Thursday [____] – I will focus less on what I can get and more on what I can give

_____

_____

_____

_____

_____

Friday [____] – Happiness is a choice and I will make the choice to be happy

_____

_____

_____

_____

_____

Saturday [____] – Today I will do the things that I have been putting off

_____

_____

_____

_____

_____

Sunday [____] – I become more valuable by adding value to the lives of others

_____

_____

_____

_____

_____

[Weekly Review] What were my accomplishments and disappointments? What commitments will I make NOW to ensure that I improve next week?

_____

_____

_____

_____

_____

→**Top Weekly Goals/Commitments** – The top 3-5 goals that I am 100% committed to achieving this week are:

_____

_____

_____

_____

_____

_____

The Life S.A.V.E.R.S. Mark each practice that you complete each day.

		M	T	W	Th	F	S	S
⇒	Silence	☐	☐	☐	☐	☐	☐	☐
⇒	Affirmations	☐	☐	☐	☐	☐	☐	☐
⇒	Visualization	☐	☐	☐	☐	☐	☐	☐
⇒	Exercise	☐	☐	☐	☐	☐	☐	☐
⇒	Reading	☐	☐	☐	☐	☐	☐	☐
⇒	Scribing	☐	☐	☐	☐	☐	☐	☐

Monday [_____] – Today is going to be my day

_____

_____

_____

_____

_____

Tuesday [_____] – My life will be in perfect harmony because I will be consciously aware of all that I am grateful for

_____

_____

_____

_____

_____

Wednesday [_____] – I expect and deserve the best

_____

_____

_____

_____

_____

Thursday [____] – Each day will bring opportunities for me to achieve

_____

_____

_____

_____

_____

_____

Friday [____] – I will gain a new perspective today by, simply, changing my environment

_____

_____

_____

_____

_____

_____

Saturday [____] – I will make today the best day possible

_____

_____

_____

_____

_____

_____

Sunday [____] – I will live well, laugh often, and love much

_____

_____

_____

_____

_____

_____

[Weekly Review] What were my accomplishments and disappointments? What commitments will I make NOW to ensure that I improve next week?

_____

_____

_____

_____

_____

_____

→**Top Weekly Goals/Commitments** – The top 3-5 goals that I am 100% committed to achieving this week are:

_____
_____
_____
_____
_____

The Life S.A.V.E.R.S. Mark each practice that you complete each day.

⇒ Silence.............................. ☐ M ☐ T ☐ W ☐ Th ☐ F ☐ S ☐ S
⇒ Affirmations................ ☐ M ☐ T ☐ W ☐ Th ☐ F ☐ S ☐ S
⇒ Visualization................ ☐ M ☐ T ☐ W ☐ Th ☐ F ☐ S ☐ S
⇒ Exercise........................... ☐ M ☐ T ☐ W ☐ Th ☐ F ☐ S ☐ S
⇒ Reading............................ ☐ M ☐ T ☐ W ☐ Th ☐ F ☐ S ☐ S
⇒ Scribing........................... ☐ M ☐ T ☐ W ☐ Th ☐ F ☐ S ☐ S

Monday [____] – Today I will seize the day, not snooze the day

_____
_____
_____
_____
_____

Tuesday [____] – I will learn by listening more and talking less

_____
_____
_____
_____
_____

Wednesday [____] – I will do everything I say I will do without exceptions or excuses

_____
_____
_____
_____
_____

Thursday [_____] – I will wake up today with passion, purpose, and a plan

_____
_____
_____
_____
_____
_____

Friday [_____] – I will say it over and over until I believe it, and then I will become it

_____
_____
_____
_____
_____
_____

Saturday [_____] – Use the evidence of what others have accomplished as proof that you can too

_____
_____
_____
_____
_____
_____

Sunday [_____] – I will stay calm in the face of difficult situations

_____
_____
_____
_____
_____
_____

[Weekly Review] What were my accomplishments and disappointments? What commitments will I make NOW to ensure that I improve next week?

_____
_____
_____
_____
_____
_____

➔**Top Weekly Goals/Commitments** – The top 3-5 goals that I am 100% committed to achieving this week are:

_____

_____

_____

_____

_____

The Life S.A.V.E.R.S. Mark each practice that you complete each day.

⇒ Silence........................... ☐ M ☐ T ☐ W ☐ Th ☐ F ☐ S ☐ S
⇒ Affirmations................. ☐ M ☐ T ☐ W ☐ Th ☐ F ☐ S ☐ S
⇒ Visualization................. ☐ M ☐ T ☐ W ☐ Th ☐ F ☐ S ☐ S
⇒ Exercise.......................... ☐ M ☐ T ☐ W ☐ Th ☐ F ☐ S ☐ S
⇒ Reading........................... ☐ M ☐ T ☐ W ☐ Th ☐ F ☐ S ☐ S
⇒ Scribing........................... ☐ M ☐ T ☐ W ☐ Th ☐ F ☐ S ☐ S

Monday [____] – My positive attitude will bring great achievements

_____

_____

_____

_____

_____

Tuesday [____] – I will take time to relax

_____

_____

_____

_____

_____

Wednesday [____] – I will not be stuck on where to start, but will instead focus on taking the first step

_____

_____

_____

_____

_____

Thursday [____] – I will put myself in situations where energy is required to increase my own energy

_____
_____
_____
_____
_____
_____

Friday [____] – I will make time to do the important things

_____
_____
_____
_____
_____

Saturday [____] – I will share my vision with others

_____
_____
_____
_____
_____

Sunday [____] – I will devote the majority of my time, energy, and attention toward living my purpose

_____
_____
_____
_____
_____

[Weekly Review] What were my accomplishments and disappointments? What commitments will I make NOW to ensure that I improve next week?

_____
_____
_____
_____
_____

→Top Weekly Goals/Commitments – The top 3-5 goals that I am 100% committed to achieving this week are:

_____

_____

_____

_____

_____

The Life S.A.V.E.R.S. Mark each practice that you complete each day.

⇒ Silence............................ ☐ M ☐ T ☐ W ☐ Th ☐ F ☐ S ☐ S
⇒ Affirmations................ ☐ M ☐ T ☐ W ☐ Th ☐ F ☐ S ☐ S
⇒ Visualization................ ☐ M ☐ T ☐ W ☐ Th ☐ F ☐ S ☐ S
⇒ Exercise.......................... ☐ M ☐ T ☐ W ☐ Th ☐ F ☐ S ☐ S
⇒ Reading.......................... ☐ M ☐ T ☐ W ☐ Th ☐ F ☐ S ☐ S
⇒ Scribing.......................... ☐ M ☐ T ☐ W ☐ Th ☐ F ☐ S ☐ S

Monday [_____] – I will focus less on what I think I know so that there is more space for me to learn and grow

_____

_____

_____

_____

_____

Tuesday [_____] – I will be in harmony with all of life

_____

_____

_____

_____

Wednesday [_____] – My life is a wonderful adventure

_____

_____

_____

_____

Thursday [____] – I will accept all things that I can't change, be grateful for all that I have, and constantly create progress towards my goals and dreams

_____
_____
_____
_____
_____
_____

Friday [____] – I will plan my life and live my plan

_____
_____
_____
_____
_____

Saturday [____] – I will be responsible for the quality of my life

_____
_____
_____
_____
_____

Sunday [____] – I will forever be happy never be content, and always know the difference

_____
_____
_____
_____
_____

[Weekly Review] What were my accomplishments and disappointments? What commitments will I make NOW to ensure that I improve next week?

_____
_____
_____
_____
_____

→**Top Weekly Goals/Commitments** – The top 3-5 goals that I am 100% committed to achieving this week are:

_____

_____

_____

_____

_____

The Life S.A.V.E.R.S. Mark each practice that you complete each day.
⇒ Silence............................ ☐ M ☐ T ☐ W ☐ Th ☐ F ☐ S ☐ S
⇒ Affirmations............... ☐ M ☐ T ☐ W ☐ Th ☐ F ☐ S ☐ S
⇒ Visualization................ ☐ M ☐ T ☐ W ☐ Th ☐ F ☐ S ☐ S
⇒ Exercise........................ ☐ M ☐ T ☐ W ☐ Th ☐ F ☐ S ☐ S
⇒ Reading......................... ☐ M ☐ T ☐ W ☐ Th ☐ F ☐ S ☐ S
⇒ Scribing........................ ☐ M ☐ T ☐ W ☐ Th ☐ F ☐ S ☐ S

Monday [____] – I will accept life before it happens

_____

_____

_____

_____

_____

Tuesday [____] – I will discipline myself to save money

_____

_____

_____

_____

_____

Wednesday [____] – I will devote one day per week to fun and relaxation

_____

_____

_____

_____

_____

Thursday [____] – I always have a winning attitude

Friday [____] – I will choose to see today as the best day of my life because what's going on around me is not as important as what's going on inside of me

---

Saturday [____] – I will not only learn something today, but I will live it

---

Sunday [____] – I will be responsible for choosing the most empowering reasons for the occurrences of my life

---

[Weekly Review] What were my accomplishments and disappointments? What commitments will I make NOW to ensure that I improve next week?

→**Top Weekly Goals/Commitments** – The top 3-5 goals that I am 100% committed to achieving this week are:

_____

_____

_____

_____

_____

_____

The Life S.A.V.E.R.S. Mark each practice that you complete each day.							
⇒ Silence...........................	☐ M	☐ T	☐ W	☐ Th	☐ F	☐ S	☐ S
⇒ Affirmations.................	☐ M	☐ T	☐ W	☐ Th	☐ F	☐ S	☐ S
⇒ Visualization................	☐ M	☐ T	☐ W	☐ Th	☐ F	☐ S	☐ S
⇒ Exercise........................	☐ M	☐ T	☐ W	☐ Th	☐ F	☐ S	☐ S
⇒ Reading.........................	☐ M	☐ T	☐ W	☐ Th	☐ F	☐ S	☐ S
⇒ Scribing........................	☐ M	☐ T	☐ W	☐ Th	☐ F	☐ S	☐ S

Monday [____] – I will maintain unwavering faith in my dreams and give extraordinary effort toward my goals to create miracles in my life

_____

_____

_____

_____

_____

Tuesday [____] – I will always have a winning attitude

_____

_____

_____

_____

_____

Wednesday [____] – I am thankful for the abundance that is mine

_____

_____

_____

_____

_____

Thursday [_____] – I will focus less on what I can get and more on what I can give

_____
_____
_____
_____
_____
_____

Friday [_____] – I will help others to be successful

_____
_____
_____
_____
_____
_____

Saturday [_____] – I will put forth extraordinary effort to produce extraordinary results

_____
_____
_____
_____
_____
_____

Sunday [_____] – I will meet all challenges with determination

_____
_____
_____
_____
_____
_____

[Weekly Review] What were my accomplishments and disappointments? What commitments will I make NOW to ensure that I improve next week?

_____
_____
_____
_____
_____
_____

➔**Top Weekly Goals/Commitments** – The top 3-5 goals that I am 100% committed to achieving this week are:

_____

_____

_____

_____

_____

The Life S.A.V.E.R.S. Mark each practice that you complete each day.

⇒	Silence	☐ M ☐ T ☐ W ☐ Th ☐ F ☐ S ☐ S
⇒	Affirmations	☐ M ☐ T ☐ W ☐ Th ☐ F ☐ S ☐ S
⇒	Visualization	☐ M ☐ T ☐ W ☐ Th ☐ F ☐ S ☐ S
⇒	Exercise	☐ M ☐ T ☐ W ☐ Th ☐ F ☐ S ☐ S
⇒	Reading	☐ M ☐ T ☐ W ☐ Th ☐ F ☐ S ☐ S
⇒	Scribing	☐ M ☐ T ☐ W ☐ Th ☐ F ☐ S ☐ S

Monday [_____] – I will value my integrity at the highest level, live in alignment with my word, and follow through with my commitments

_____

_____

_____

_____

_____

_____

Tuesday [_____] – I will learn to manage stress to achieve a happier life

_____

_____

_____

_____

_____

Wednesday [_____] – I will anticipate and plan ahead to meet challenges

_____

_____

_____

_____

_____

_____

Thursday [_____] – My personal growth is about progress, not perfection

_____

_____

_____

_____

_____

Friday [_____] – I will love the life I have while I create the best life I can imagine

_____

_____

_____

_____

_____

Saturday – My mind will grow stronger through use

_____

_____

_____

_____

Sunday [_____] – How I think will determine how I act

_____

_____

_____

_____

_____

[Weekly Review] What did I accomplish, learn, or realize this week? What new commitments will I make NOW to ensure this next week is even better?

_____

_____

_____

_____

_____

➜Top Weekly Goals/Commitments – The top 3-5 goals that I am 100% committed to achieving this week are:

_____

_____

_____

_____

_____

The Life S.A.V.E.R.S. Mark each practice that you complete each day.

		M	T	W	Th	F	S	S
⇒	Silence............................	☐	☐	☐	☐	☐	☐	☐
⇒	Affirmations................	☐	☐	☐	☐	☐	☐	☐
⇒	Visualization................	☐	☐	☐	☐	☐	☐	☐
⇒	Exercise..........................	☐	☐	☐	☐	☐	☐	☐
⇒	Reading...........................	☐	☐	☐	☐	☐	☐	☐
⇒	Scribing..........................	☐	☐	☐	☐	☐	☐	☐

Monday [_____] – I am focused and animated

_____

_____

_____

_____

_____

Tuesday [_____] – I will think about what I want to invite into my life

_____

_____

_____

_____

_____

Wednesday [_____] – Each day I will expect the best of myself and accept the rest from myself

_____

_____

_____

_____

_____

Thursday [____] – My empowering perspective will give birth to my empowered life

_____
_____
_____
_____
_____
_____

Friday [____] – I believe that I am better every day

_____
_____
_____
_____
_____

Saturday [____] – Every day I wake up, I will create intention and then commit to making it my best day ever

_____
_____
_____
_____
_____

Sunday [____] – I will contribute to my community

_____
_____
_____
_____
_____

[Weekly Review] What did I accomplish, learn, or realize this week? What new commitments will I make NOW to ensure this next week is even better?

_____
_____
_____
_____
_____

→**Top Weekly Goals/Commitments** – The top 3-5 goals that I am 100% committed to achieving this week are:

_____
_____
_____
_____
_____

The Life S.A.V.E.R.S. Mark each practice that you complete each day.

⇒ Silence.............................. ☐ M ☐ T ☐ W ☐ Th ☐ F ☐ S ☐ S
⇒ Affirmations.................. ☐ M ☐ T ☐ W ☐ Th ☐ F ☐ S ☐ S
⇒ Visualization................. ☐ M ☐ T ☐ W ☐ Th ☐ F ☐ S ☐ S
⇒ Exercise........................... ☐ M ☐ T ☐ W ☐ Th ☐ F ☐ S ☐ S
⇒ Reading............................ ☐ M ☐ T ☐ W ☐ Th ☐ F ☐ S ☐ S
⇒ Scribing........................... ☐ M ☐ T ☐ W ☐ Th ☐ F ☐ S ☐ S

Monday [____] – I will set goals that are BOLD enough to scare me, but inspiring and exciting enough for me to commit 100% to

_____
_____
_____
_____
_____

Tuesday [____] – I will stop rebelling against living my life to the fullest

_____
_____
_____
_____
_____

Wednesday [____] – I am worthy of success and have paid my dues

_____
_____
_____
_____
_____

Thursday [_____] – I will tell myself, "Life is perfect and I am grateful" and repeat it until I believe it

_____
_____
_____
_____
_____
_____

Friday [_____] – I believe I am better every day

_____
_____
_____
_____
_____

Saturday [_____] – I will give more than I get every day, everywhere, with everyone, always

_____
_____
_____
_____
_____

Sunday [_____] – I look for opportunities to grow

_____
_____
_____
_____
_____

[Weekly Review] What did I accomplish, learn, or realize this week? What new commitments will I make NOW to ensure this next week is even better?

_____
_____
_____
_____
_____

→Top Weekly Goals/Commitments – The top 3-5 goals that I am 100% committed to achieving this week are:

_____

_____

_____

_____

_____

The Life S.A.V.E.R.S. Mark each practice that you complete each day.

		M	T	W	Th	F	S	S
⇒	Silence............................	☐	☐	☐	☐	☐	☐	☐
⇒	Affirmations................	☐	☐	☐	☐	☐	☐	☐
⇒	Visualization................	☐	☐	☐	☐	☐	☐	☐
⇒	Exercise..........................	☐	☐	☐	☐	☐	☐	☐
⇒	Reading..........................	☐	☐	☐	☐	☐	☐	☐
⇒	Scribing..........................	☐	☐	☐	☐	☐	☐	☐

Monday [_____] – I am thankful for the people in my life who have guided and supported me

_____

_____

_____

_____

_____

Tuesday [_____] – I am what I choose to be

_____

_____

_____

_____

_____

Wednesday [_____] – My enthusiasm will lead to great achievements

_____

_____

_____

_____

_____

Thursday [_____] – I must embrace that I am already perfect as I am and everything else is just a story that I tell myself

_____

_____

_____

_____

_____

Friday [_____] – I will cheerfully give people more than they expect

_____

_____

_____

_____

_____

Saturday [_____] – My current life situation is the perfect opportunity for me to learn, grow, and become better that I've ever been before

_____

_____

_____

_____

_____

Sunday [_____] – There is no limit to what I can learn

_____

_____

_____

_____

_____

[Weekly Review] What did I accomplish, learn, or realize this week? What new commitments will I make NOW to ensure this next week is even better?

_____

_____

_____

_____

_____

➔**Top Weekly Goals/Commitments** – The top 3-5 goals that I am 100% committed to achieving this week are:

_____

_____

_____

_____

_____

The Life S.A.V.E.R.S. Mark each practice that you complete each day.

⇒ Silence.............................. ☐ M ☐ T ☐ W ☐ Th ☐ F ☐ S ☐ S
⇒ Affirmations............... ☐ M ☐ T ☐ W ☐ Th ☐ F ☐ S ☐ S
⇒ Visualization................ ☐ M ☐ T ☐ W ☐ Th ☐ F ☐ S ☐ S
⇒ Exercise......................... ☐ M ☐ T ☐ W ☐ Th ☐ F ☐ S ☐ S
⇒ Reading.......................... ☐ M ☐ T ☐ W ☐ Th ☐ F ☐ S ☐ S
⇒ Scribing.......................... ☐ M ☐ T ☐ W ☐ Th ☐ F ☐ S ☐ S

Monday [____] – My upward climb will be easier when I take people with me

_____

_____

_____

_____

_____

Tuesday [____] – My positive thoughts will grow stronger with repetition

_____

_____

_____

_____

_____

Wednesday [____] – I have the power to change my life

_____

_____

_____

_____

_____

Thursday [_____] – I am ready for the greater good in my life

_____
_____
_____
_____
_____
_____

Friday [_____] – I will prioritize and focus my time on what will have the greatest positive impact on my life right now

_____
_____
_____
_____
_____
_____

Saturday [_____] – I know how to use my time effectively

_____
_____
_____
_____
_____
_____

Sunday [_____] – I am genuinely interested in other people

_____
_____
_____
_____
_____
_____

[Weekly Review] What did I accomplish, learn, or realize this week? What new commitments will I make NOW to ensure this next week is even better?

_____
_____
_____
_____
_____
_____

```
┌─────────────────────────────────────────┐
│                                         │
│      The Miracle Morning Journal        │
│        — 6-MONTH REVIEW —               │
│                                         │
└─────────────────────────────────────────┘
```

Can you believe the year is already halfway over?! Time definitely flies when you're creating and living an extraordinary life… ☺

Now it's time to evaluate the first 6 months of your year by answering 4 simple, but powerful questions. This powerful process will allow you to capitalize on the first six months of your year by increasing your self-awareness, so that you can make adjustments and improvements to ensure that the next six months are up to 10X (yes—10 times) better than the previous six!

This exercise is so important that I recommend scheduling a few hours to flip back to your first entry in your *Miracle Morning* Journal and relive your entire year as you come back to this page to answer the 4 "My Better Half" Questions below. Go ahead, and get started now. Or if now is not a good time, please put it in your schedule to do as soon as possible…

Your 4 "My Better Half" Questions To Ensure That the Next 6 Months of the Year Are Your BEST 6 Months of the Year!

What if I told you there are four simple, but life-changing questions that you could ask yourself right now, and the answers would virtually guarantee that you see dramatic improvements in your life during the next 6 months? I'm talking about your becoming the best version of yourself—personally, professionally, financially, physically, mentally, emotionally, you name it. Would you invest the time to answer those 4 questions?

4 Questions to Take Your Life to the Next Level In the Next 6 Months:

I'm about to give you four strategic questions that you can ask and answer for yourself today, which will help ensure that you're able to make the rest of your year the BEST of your year. That is why I call them your "My Better Half" Questions. In fact, these four questions are SO valuable, that the first time I did this exercise (in 2008), the answers I came up were so impactful that they inspired me to spend an entire weekend reflecting on my answers. (Note: you can answer these questions in <u>10 minutes</u> or 10 hours, so don't feel like you *have to* spend the whole weekend on them, like I did.)

Here are your 4 *My Better Half Questions*, followed by a few specific action steps you can take in the next few days that will help you ensure that you implement the value you gain from this exercise:

1. What did I accomplish?
2. What were my biggest disappointments?
3. What valuable lessons can I learn from each?
4. What are my "Top 3" Guidelines for the 2nd half of the year?

Q1 – What did I accomplish?

Unfortunately, most of us find it easier and tend to spend more time and energy dwelling on our failures and disappointments than we do acknowledging our successes and accomplishments. But all of us have *both*, and dwelling on our failures and what we 'didn't get accomplished' only discourages us and hurts our self-confidence.

It is only by acknowledging our accomplishments that we improve our self-image, raise our self-esteem, increase our self-confidence and empower ourselves to accomplish more in the future.

The first time I answered this question, and wrote down as many of my accomplishments as I could think of (big ones & small ones) I got to 42, and the perception I had of the first half of my year started to change. I realized that I wasn't as behind as I had been telling myself I was. I gave myself permission to actually *feel good* about all that I accomplished. I actually closed my eyes, smiled, and said to myself over and over, "You're doing great this year, Hal... You're doing great this year, Hal!" This may sound funny, but it felt so good to simply spend time acknowledging myself for once, for all that I had accomplished! Try it; I think you'll be pleasantly surprised by the results.

_____

_____

_____

_____

_____

_____

_____

_____

_____

Q2 – What were my biggest disappointments?

While it is neither necessary nor particularly healthy to beat ourselves up about our disappointments, it IS important and proactive to acknowledge our disappointments so that we can learn from them and let them go. How did we let ourselves or others down last year? What goals did we fail to achieve? What bad habits did we continue?

Disappointments are a part of life, and we all have them. As long as we learn from our disappointments, we can use them to help us grow and improve so that we don't continue to make them in the future. As you review the first six months of this year, what were your biggest disappointments?

_____

_____

_____

_____

_____

_____

_____

_____

_____

Q3 – What valuable lessons can I learn from each?

One lesson I have implemented that continues to empower me to improve every area of my life is to, *"Learn something from everything."* When it comes to learning from our 'accomplishments' we can take away valuable lessons related to what it was that motivated, inspired, or allowed us to accomplish what we accomplished. As for learning from our disappointments, we can internalize valuable lessons about which thoughts, behaviors, actions, emotions, or habits prompted us to create or to not create that which disappointed us. Usually it is our biggest disappointments that can provide us with our most life-changing lessons.

_____

_____

_____

_____

_____

_____

_____

Q4 – What are my "Top 3" Success Guidelines for the next 6 months?

Once you have acknowledged your accomplishments and your disappointments, and you've extracted the most valuable, life-enhancing LESSONS from each, what may benefit you the most is choosing your "Top 3" guidelines to keep you on track during the coming year. You can simply copy and paste your 3 most empowering lessons, and post these up somewhere that you will look at them every day to stay focused on that which will make the biggest impact on improving your life next year and beyond.

Here are the Top 3 Success Guidelines that I came up with in 2008:

1. Focus on one project (or task) at a time and complete it, before moving onto the next.
2. Delegate all tasks that don't compliment my natural gifts and unique areas of brilliance.
3. Make everything I do FUN and done with unconditional LOVE and authentic GRATITUDE.

So, what are your Top 3 Success Guidelines for the next 6 months?

1. _____

_____

_____

2. _____

_____

_____

3. _____

_____

_____

Final Thoughts: I hope you've made the decision to invest time into answering these 4 "My Better Half" Questions. You'll have an opportunity to answer them again in six months during your *Miracle Morning* Journal "ANNUAL REVIEW." Here's to making the next 6 months, your BEST 6 months!

➔**Top Weekly Goals/Commitments** – The top 3-5 goals that I am 100% committed to achieving this week are:

_____

_____

_____

_____

_____

The **Life S.A.V.E.R.S.** Mark each practice that you complete each day.

		M	T	W	Th	F	S	S
⇒	Silence	☐	☐	☐	☐	☐	☐	☐
⇒	Affirmations	☐	☐	☐	☐	☐	☐	☐
⇒	Visualization	☐	☐	☐	☐	☐	☐	☐
⇒	Exercise	☐	☐	☐	☐	☐	☐	☐
⇒	Reading	☐	☐	☐	☐	☐	☐	☐
⇒	Scribing	☐	☐	☐	☐	☐	☐	☐

Monday [____] – I will rise above human nature and tap into the SUPER-human that is within each of us

_____

_____

_____

_____

_____

_____

Tuesday [____] – I can and I will

_____

_____

_____

_____

_____

Wednesday [____] – I open my own doors of opportunity

_____

_____

_____

_____

_____

_____

Thursday [____] – I develop clear positive values that guide my choices

_____

_____

_____

_____

_____

Friday [____] – I will learn to like what I usually resist by simply doing it consistently

_____

_____

_____

_____

_____

Saturday [____] – What I do with these precious moments today, will create my tomorrow

_____

_____

_____

_____

_____

Sunday [____] – Everyone is my teacher

_____

_____

_____

_____

_____

[Weekly Review] What did I accomplish, learn, or realize this week? What new commitments will I make NOW to ensure this next week is even better?

_____

_____

_____

_____

_____

→**Top Weekly Goals/Commitments** – The top 3-5 goals that I am 100% committed to achieving this week are:

_____

_____

_____

_____

_____

The Life S.A.V.E.R.S. Mark each practice that you complete each day.

⇒ Silence............................. ☐ M ☐ T ☐ W ☐ Th ☐ F ☐ S ☐ S
⇒ Affirmations................ ☐ M ☐ T ☐ W ☐ Th ☐ F ☐ S ☐ S
⇒ Visualization.............. ☐ M ☐ T ☐ W ☐ Th ☐ F ☐ S ☐ S
⇒ Exercise......................... ☐ M ☐ T ☐ W ☐ Th ☐ F ☐ S ☐ S
⇒ Reading.......................... ☐ M ☐ T ☐ W ☐ Th ☐ F ☐ S ☐ S
⇒ Scribing......................... ☐ M ☐ T ☐ W ☐ Th ☐ F ☐ S ☐ S

Monday [____] – I will treat everyone with love and respect

_____

_____

_____

_____

_____

Tuesday [____] – I will always expect the best of myself

_____

_____

_____

_____

_____

Wednesday [____] – I will choose wisely and live intelligently

_____

_____

_____

_____

_____

Thursday [____] – I will choose the abundant life

_____
_____
_____
_____
_____

Friday [____] – I will practice what makes me happy until it becomes a habit

_____
_____
_____
_____
_____

Saturday [____] – It is my responsibility to create motivation daily

_____
_____
_____
_____
_____

Sunday [____] – I will nourish my mind, body, and spirit today and every day

_____
_____
_____
_____
_____

[Weekly Review] What were my accomplishments and disappointments? What commitments will I make NOW to ensure that I improve next week?

_____
_____
_____
_____
_____

➔**Top Weekly Goals/Commitments** – The top 3-5 goals that I am 100% committed to achieving this week are:

_____

_____

_____

_____

_____

The Life S.A.V.E.R.S. Mark each practice that you complete each day.

		M	T	W	Th	F	S	S
⇒	Silence............................	☐	☐	☐	☐	☐	☐	☐
⇒	Affirmations................	☐	☐	☐	☐	☐	☐	☐
⇒	Visualization................	☐	☐	☐	☐	☐	☐	☐
⇒	Exercise..........................	☐	☐	☐	☐	☐	☐	☐
⇒	Reading...........................	☐	☐	☐	☐	☐	☐	☐
⇒	Scribing..........................	☐	☐	☐	☐	☐	☐	☐

Monday [_____] – I will enjoy life to the fullest

_____

_____

_____

_____

_____

Tuesday [_____] – I will be excited about the possibility of achieving my goals

_____

_____

_____

_____

_____

Wednesday [_____] – Today is the best day to do the things that I have been putting off.

_____

_____

_____

_____

_____

Thursday [____] – I will take the necessary actions today to change my life

_____

_____

_____

_____

_____

Friday [____] – I get out of life what I put into it

_____

_____

_____

_____

_____

Saturday [____] – Today, I will master my ability to get started. I will take the first step towards something I've been putting off doing

_____

_____

_____

_____

_____

Sunday [____] – I deserve to be proud of myself

_____

_____

_____

_____

_____

[Weekly Review] What were my accomplishments and disappointments? What commitments will I make NOW to ensure that I improve next week?

_____

_____

_____

_____

_____

➔Top Weekly Goals/Commitments – The top 3-5 goals that I am 100% committed to achieving this week are:

_____

_____

_____

_____

_____

The Life S.A.V.E.R.S. Mark each practice that you complete each day.

⇒ Silence.............................. ☐ M ☐ T ☐ W ☐ Th ☐ F ☐ S ☐ S
⇒ Affirmations................ ☐ M ☐ T ☐ W ☐ Th ☐ F ☐ S ☐ S
⇒ Visualization................ ☐ M ☐ T ☐ W ☐ Th ☐ F ☐ S ☐ S
⇒ Exercise........................... ☐ M ☐ T ☐ W ☐ Th ☐ F ☐ S ☐ S
⇒ Reading............................ ☐ M ☐ T ☐ W ☐ Th ☐ F ☐ S ☐ S
⇒ Scribing........................... ☐ M ☐ T ☐ W ☐ Th ☐ F ☐ S ☐ S

Monday [____] – I will not avoid them, but welcome changes and challenges

_____

_____

_____

_____

_____

Tuesday [____] – I expect the best, and I accept the rest

_____

_____

_____

_____

_____

Wednesday [____] – I develop my character through the unwavering pursuit of my goals

_____

_____

_____

_____

_____

Thursday [____] – I focus on my strengths

_____
_____
_____
_____
_____
_____

Friday [____] – I work with purpose and passion towards my vision

_____
_____
_____
_____
_____
_____

Saturday [____] – It is who I become that matters

_____
_____
_____
_____
_____
_____

Sunday [____] – I will become a champion by thinking and talking like a champion.

_____
_____
_____
_____
_____
_____

[Weekly Review] What were my accomplishments and disappointments? What commitments will I make NOW to ensure that I improve next week?

_____
_____
_____
_____
_____
_____

→**Top Weekly Goals/Commitments** – The top 3-5 goals that I am 100% committed to achieving this week are:

_____
_____
_____
_____
_____

The Life S.A.V.E.R.S. Mark each practice that you complete each day.

⇒ Silence........................... ☐ M ☐ T ☐ W ☐ Th ☐ F ☐ S ☐ S
⇒ Affirmations............... ☐ M ☐ T ☐ W ☐ Th ☐ F ☐ S ☐ S
⇒ Visualization............... ☐ M ☐ T ☐ W ☐ Th ☐ F ☐ S ☐ S
⇒ Exercise......................... ☐ M ☐ T ☐ W ☐ Th ☐ F ☐ S ☐ S
⇒ Reading........................... ☐ M ☐ T ☐ W ☐ Th ☐ F ☐ S ☐ S
⇒ Scribing........................... ☐ M ☐ T ☐ W ☐ Th ☐ F ☐ S ☐ S

Monday [_____] – I always look to better my best and go to the next level

_____
_____
_____
_____
_____

Tuesday [_____] – I am open to new experiences and seek new challenges

_____
_____
_____
_____
_____

Wednesday [_____] – Whatever I want in life is available to me

_____
_____
_____
_____
_____

Thursday [____] – The universe is just waiting for me to take action

_____
_____
_____
_____
_____
_____

Friday [____] – I am committed to being the most positive person I know

_____
_____
_____
_____
_____
_____

Saturday [____] – This morning I will choose to be open to new ideas and opportunities

_____
_____
_____
_____
_____
_____

Sunday [____] – I will dedicate my day to learning, growing, connecting, and contributing with every person I come in contact with

_____
_____
_____
_____
_____
_____

[Weekly Review] What were my accomplishments and disappointments? What commitments will I make NOW to ensure that I improve next week?

_____
_____
_____
_____
_____
_____

→Top Weekly Goals/Commitments – The top 3-5 goals that I am 100% committed to achieving this week are:

_____

_____

_____

_____

_____

The Life S.A.V.E.R.S. Mark each practice that you complete each day.

⇒ Silence............................ ☐ M ☐ T ☐ W ☐ Th ☐ F ☐ S ☐ S
⇒ Affirmations................. ☐ M ☐ T ☐ W ☐ Th ☐ F ☐ S ☐ S
⇒ Visualization................ ☐ M ☐ T ☐ W ☐ Th ☐ F ☐ S ☐ S
⇒ Exercise......................... ☐ M ☐ T ☐ W ☐ Th ☐ F ☐ S ☐ S
⇒ Reading.......................... ☐ M ☐ T ☐ W ☐ Th ☐ F ☐ S ☐ S
⇒ Scribing.......................... ☐ M ☐ T ☐ W ☐ Th ☐ F ☐ S ☐ S

Monday [_____] – I am shaped by the company I keep so I will surround myself with inspired company

_____

_____

_____

_____

_____

Tuesday [_____] – I will keep my mind focused on what I want

_____

_____

_____

_____

Wednesday [_____] – I am responsible for who I am and where I'm going

_____

_____

_____

_____

_____

Thursday [____] – I will be a force for good, a force for creation, and a force for selfless contribution

_____

_____

_____

_____

_____

_____

Friday – I visualize myself exactly the way I want to be

_____

_____

_____

_____

_____

_____

Saturday [____] – I will not judge myself through others' eyes

_____

_____

_____

_____

_____

_____

Sunday [____] – I have decided that today is going to be an amazing day, and if it is to be, it is up to me

_____

_____

_____

_____

_____

_____

[Weekly Review] What were my accomplishments and disappointments? What commitments will I make NOW to ensure that I improve next week?

_____

_____

_____

_____

_____

➔**Top Weekly Goals/Commitments** – The top 3-5 goals that I am 100% committed to achieving this week are:

_____
_____
_____
_____
_____

The Life S.A.V.E.R.S. Mark each practice that you complete each day.

⇒ Silence............................ ☐ M ☐ T ☐ W ☐ Th ☐ F ☐ S ☐ S
⇒ Affirmations............... ☐ M ☐ T ☐ W ☐ Th ☐ F ☐ S ☐ S
⇒ Visualization............... ☐ M ☐ T ☐ W ☐ Th ☐ F ☐ S ☐ S
⇒ Exercise......................... ☐ M ☐ T ☐ W ☐ Th ☐ F ☐ S ☐ S
⇒ Reading.......................... ☐ M ☐ T ☐ W ☐ Th ☐ F ☐ S ☐ S
⇒ Scribing.......................... ☐ M ☐ T ☐ W ☐ Th ☐ F ☐ S ☐ S

Monday [_____] – I believe I am worthy of all the good things that I desire

_____
_____
_____
_____
_____

Tuesday [_____] – Today, I will no longer justify mediocrity in my life. Today and from now on, I am capable of achieving anything

_____
_____
_____
_____
_____

Wednesday [_____] – I pursue excellence in everything I do

_____
_____
_____
_____
_____

Thursday [____] – I take pride in doing my job to the best of my abilities

_____
_____
_____
_____
_____
_____

Friday [____] – I am forgiving of myself and others

_____
_____
_____
_____
_____
_____

Saturday [____] – I will give up who I've been for who I want to become

_____
_____
_____
_____
_____
_____

Sunday [____] – I will move in the direction of my goals and dreams, even when I don't feel like it

_____
_____
_____
_____
_____
_____

[Weekly Review] What were my accomplishments and disappointments? What commitments will I make NOW to ensure that I improve next week?

_____
_____
_____
_____
_____
_____

➔Top Weekly Goals/Commitments – The top 3-5 goals that I am 100% committed to achieving this week are:

_____

_____

_____

_____

_____

The Life S.A.V.E.R.S. Mark each practice that you complete each day.

⇒ Silence............................ ☐ M ☐ T ☐ W ☐ Th ☐ F ☐ S ☐ S
⇒ Affirmations.............. ☐ M ☐ T ☐ W ☐ Th ☐ F ☐ S ☐ S
⇒ Visualization............... ☐ M ☐ T ☐ W ☐ Th ☐ F ☐ S ☐ S
⇒ Exercise........................ ☐ M ☐ T ☐ W ☐ Th ☐ F ☐ S ☐ S
⇒ Reading.......................... ☐ M ☐ T ☐ W ☐ Th ☐ F ☐ S ☐ S
⇒ Scribing......................... ☐ M ☐ T ☐ W ☐ Th ☐ F ☐ S ☐ S

Monday [____] – I am forgiving of myself and others

_____

_____

_____

_____

Tuesday [____] – I will not accept less from myself than I can be

_____

_____

_____

_____

_____

Wednesday [____] – To have more, I will be more

_____

_____

_____

_____

_____

Thursday [____] – When I am unmotivated I will take a step of action to fuel my motivation

_____
_____
_____
_____
_____

Friday [____] – I alter my situation by changing my belief

_____
_____
_____
_____
_____

Saturday [____] – I will change my thoughts to change my life

_____
_____
_____
_____
_____

Sunday [____] – I will expect a miracle in my life today

_____
_____
_____
_____
_____

[Weekly Review] What were my accomplishments and disappointments? What commitments will I make NOW to ensure that I improve next week?

_____
_____
_____
_____
_____

→**Top Weekly Goals/Commitments** – The top 3-5 goals that I am 100% committed to achieving this week are:

_____
_____
_____
_____
_____

The Life S.A.V.E.R.S. Mark each practice that you complete each day.

		M	T	W	Th	F	S	S
⇒	Silence............................	☐	☐	☐	☐	☐	☐	☐
⇒	Affirmations...............	☐	☐	☐	☐	☐	☐	☐
⇒	Visualization...............	☐	☐	☐	☐	☐	☐	☐
⇒	Exercise........................	☐	☐	☐	☐	☐	☐	☐
⇒	Reading..........................	☐	☐	☐	☐	☐	☐	☐
⇒	Scribing.........................	☐	☐	☐	☐	☐	☐	☐

Monday [____] – I will remove all barriers from my path

_____
_____
_____
_____
_____

Tuesday [____] – I am choosing to be happy because I want to be happy

_____
_____
_____
_____
_____

Wednesday [____] – I will think BIG to make it BIG

_____
_____
_____
_____
_____

Thursday [____] – Today is the first day of the rest of my life

_____
_____
_____
_____
_____

Friday – I see many options in every situation

_____
_____
_____
_____
_____

Saturday [____] – Whether I believe I can or believe that I cannot, either way, I am right

_____
_____
_____
_____
_____

Sunday [____] – I will create my own horoscopes and forecasts

_____
_____
_____
_____
_____

[Weekly Review] What were my accomplishments and disappointments? What commitments will I make NOW to ensure that I improve next week?

_____
_____
_____
_____
_____

➔**Top Weekly Goals/Commitments** – The top 3-5 goals that I am 100% committed to achieving this week are:

_____

_____

_____

_____

_____

The Life S.A.V.E.R.S. Mark each practice that you complete each day.

		M	T	W	Th	F	S	S
⇒	Silence................................	☐	☐	☐	☐	☐	☐	☐
⇒	Affirmations.................	☐	☐	☐	☐	☐	☐	☐
⇒	Visualization................	☐	☐	☐	☐	☐	☐	☐
⇒	Exercise.............................	☐	☐	☐	☐	☐	☐	☐
⇒	Reading.............................	☐	☐	☐	☐	☐	☐	☐
⇒	Scribing.............................	☐	☐	☐	☐	☐	☐	☐

Monday [_____] – I will be more courageous today than I was yesterday

_____

_____

_____

_____

_____

Tuesday [_____] – I can add value to the life of every individual that I meet

_____

_____

_____

_____

Wednesday [_____] – I will remain passionate in everything that I do

_____

_____

_____

_____

_____

Thursday [____] – I will finish what I start

_____

_____

_____

_____

_____

Friday [____] – I will remember to be thankful for all that I have, every day

_____

_____

_____

_____

_____

Saturday [____] – I will release the past so that I am free to move forward

_____

_____

_____

_____

_____

Sunday [____] – I will strive until I succeed

_____

_____

_____

_____

_____

[Weekly Review] What were my accomplishments and disappointments? What commitments will I make NOW to ensure that I improve next week?

_____

_____

_____

_____

_____

→Top Weekly Goals/Commitments – The top 3-5 goals that I am 100% committed to achieving this week are:

_____

_____

_____

_____

_____

_____

```
The Life S.A.V.E.R.S. Mark each practice that you complete each day.
⇒   Silence...................    □ M  □ T  □ W  □ Th  □ F  □ S  □ S
⇒   Affirmations..............    □ M  □ T  □ W  □ Th  □ F  □ S  □ S
⇒   Visualization.............    □ M  □ T  □ W  □ Th  □ F  □ S  □ S
⇒   Exercise..................    □ M  □ T  □ W  □ Th  □ F  □ S  □ S
⇒   Reading...................    □ M  □ T  □ W  □ Th  □ F  □ S  □ S
⇒   Scribing..................    □ M  □ T  □ W  □ Th  □ F  □ S  □ S
```

Monday [____] – I will approach all tasks with confidence

_____

_____

_____

_____

_____

_____

Tuesday [____] – I will love deeply and passionately because there is no reward without some risk

_____

_____

_____

_____

_____

_____

Wednesday [____] – I will expect only good out of life

_____

_____

_____

_____

_____

_____

Thursday [_____] – When I find something I really want, I will not let obstacles stand in my way

_____

_____

_____

_____

_____

Friday [_____] – I will live a good and honorable life that I can be proud of, so that when I look back on it, I can enjoy it a second time

_____

_____

_____

_____

_____

Saturday [_____] – My positive energy will be infectious

_____

_____

_____

_____

_____

Sunday [_____] – I will live my life to the fullest and have no regrets

_____

_____

_____

_____

_____

[Weekly Review] What were my accomplishments and disappointments? What commitments will I make NOW to ensure that I improve next week?

_____

_____

_____

_____

_____

➔**Top Weekly Goals/Commitments** – The top 3-5 goals that I am 100% committed to achieving this week are:

_____

_____

_____

_____

_____

The Life S.A.V.E.R.S. Mark each practice that you complete each day.

⇒ Silence.............................. ☐ M ☐ T ☐ W ☐ Th ☐ F ☐ S ☐ S
⇒ Affirmations................ ☐ M ☐ T ☐ W ☐ Th ☐ F ☐ S ☐ S
⇒ Visualization................ ☐ M ☐ T ☐ W ☐ Th ☐ F ☐ S ☐ S
⇒ Exercise.......................... ☐ M ☐ T ☐ W ☐ Th ☐ F ☐ S ☐ S
⇒ Reading........................... ☐ M ☐ T ☐ W ☐ Th ☐ F ☐ S ☐ S
⇒ Scribing.......................... ☐ M ☐ T ☐ W ☐ Th ☐ F ☐ S ☐ S

Monday [_____] – I will read at least one self-improvement book each week

_____

_____

_____

_____

_____

Tuesday [_____] – I will treasure and appreciate my friends and I will express my gratitude for them

_____

_____

_____

_____

_____

Wednesday [_____] – I will surround myself with what I love

_____

_____

_____

_____

_____

Thursday [____] – I will be a role model for others and I will take the time to share my successes with those around

_____

_____

_____

_____

_____

Friday [____] – I have the power to choose my thoughts

_____

_____

_____

_____

_____

Saturday [____] – When I feel troubled, I seek support from someone that I trust and respect

_____

_____

_____

_____

_____

Sunday [____] – My words and actions always flow from good intentions

_____

_____

_____

_____

_____

[Weekly Review] What were my accomplishments and disappointments? What commitments will I make NOW to ensure that I improve next week?

_____

_____

_____

_____

_____

➔**Top Weekly Goals/Commitments** – The top 3-5 goals that I am 100% committed to achieving this week are:

_____

_____

_____

_____

_____

The Life S.A.V.E.R.S. Mark each practice that you complete each day.
⇒ Silence.......................... ☐ M ☐ T ☐ W ☐ Th ☐ F ☐ S ☐ S
⇒ Affirmations............... ☐ M ☐ T ☐ W ☐ Th ☐ F ☐ S ☐ S
⇒ Visualization.............. ☐ M ☐ T ☐ W ☐ Th ☐ F ☐ S ☐ S
⇒ Exercise....................... ☐ M ☐ T ☐ W ☐ Th ☐ F ☐ S ☐ S
⇒ Reading........................ ☐ M ☐ T ☐ W ☐ Th ☐ F ☐ S ☐ S
⇒ Scribing........................ ☐ M ☐ T ☐ W ☐ Th ☐ F ☐ S ☐ S

Monday [____] – I make a difference in the world around me

_____

_____

_____

_____

_____

_____

Tuesday [____] – My genuine feelings will inspire others

_____

_____

_____

_____

_____

_____

Wednesday [____] – I will find a reason to smile and laugh today

_____

_____

_____

_____

_____

_____

Thursday [____] – I live my life with integrity

_____
_____
_____
_____
_____
_____

Friday [____] – Peace on earth begins with me

_____
_____
_____
_____
_____
_____

Saturday [____] – I'm good enough, I'm smart enough, and doggone it, people like me

_____
_____
_____
_____
_____
_____

Sunday [____] – I have fun. Life is too short to take myself too seriously

_____
_____
_____
_____
_____
_____

[Weekly Review] What were my accomplishments and disappointments? What commitments will I make NOW to ensure that I improve next week?

_____
_____
_____
_____
_____
_____

➔**Top Weekly Goals/Commitments** – The top 3-5 goals that I am 100% committed to achieving this week are:

_____
_____
_____
_____
_____

The Life S.A.V.E.R.S. Mark each practice that you complete each day.

⇒ Silence............................ ☐ M ☐ T ☐ W ☐ Th ☐ F ☐ S ☐ S
⇒ Affirmations............... ☐ M ☐ T ☐ W ☐ Th ☐ F ☐ S ☐ S
⇒ Visualization.............. ☐ M ☐ T ☐ W ☐ Th ☐ F ☐ S ☐ S
⇒ Exercise......................... ☐ M ☐ T ☐ W ☐ Th ☐ F ☐ S ☐ S
⇒ Reading.......................... ☐ M ☐ T ☐ W ☐ Th ☐ F ☐ S ☐ S
⇒ Scribing......................... ☐ M ☐ T ☐ W ☐ Th ☐ F ☐ S ☐ S

Monday [____] – I win because I believe I can

_____
_____
_____
_____
_____

Tuesday [____] – I will not take anything in my life for granted, but rather, be mindful of all that I am grateful for

_____
_____
_____
_____
_____

Wednesday [____] – I will align my values and my goals

_____
_____
_____
_____
_____

Thursday [____] – I will make plans for the coming year to build upon the progress I have made this year

_____

_____

_____

_____

_____

_____

Friday [____] – I will always make time to make someone else's day

_____

_____

_____

_____

_____

Saturday [____] – I will be generous with my praise

_____

_____

_____

_____

_____

Sunday [____] – My dreams are within reach and I am committed to moving towards them

_____

_____

_____

_____

_____

[Weekly Review] What were my accomplishments and disappointments? What commitments will I make NOW to ensure that I improve next week?

_____

_____

_____

_____

_____

➔**Top Weekly Goals/Commitments** – The top 3-5 goals that I am 100% committed to achieving this week are:

_____
_____
_____
_____
_____

The Life S.A.V.E.R.S. Mark each practice that you complete each day.							
⇒ Silence............................	☐ M	☐ T	☐ W	☐ Th	☐ F	☐ S	☐ S
⇒ Affirmations...............	☐ M	☐ T	☐ W	☐ Th	☐ F	☐ S	☐ S
⇒ Visualization...............	☐ M	☐ T	☐ W	☐ Th	☐ F	☐ S	☐ S
⇒ Exercise..........................	☐ M	☐ T	☐ W	☐ Th	☐ F	☐ S	☐ S
⇒ Reading..........................	☐ M	☐ T	☐ W	☐ Th	☐ F	☐ S	☐ S
⇒ Scribing..........................	☐ M	☐ T	☐ W	☐ Th	☐ F	☐ S	☐ S

Monday [____] – I will embrace my mistakes because learning and growth always follow

_____
_____
_____
_____
_____

Tuesday [____] – I take risks because that is how I grow

_____
_____
_____
_____
_____

Wednesday [____] – My success starts in my mind

_____
_____
_____
_____
_____

Thursday [_____] – Everything I need to achieve anything I want is already inside of me

_____
_____
_____
_____
_____
_____

Friday [_____] – There is always room for improvement

_____
_____
_____
_____
_____
_____

Saturday [_____] – I can learn something from every individual that I encounter

_____
_____
_____
_____
_____
_____

Sunday [_____] – My environment is a mirror of my attitude

_____
_____
_____
_____
_____
_____

[Weekly Review] What were my accomplishments and disappointments? What commitments will I make NOW to ensure that I improve next week?

_____
_____
_____
_____
_____

➔**Top Weekly Goals/Commitments** – The top 3-5 goals that I am 100% committed to achieving this week are:

_____

_____

_____

_____

_____

The Life S.A.V.E.R.S. Mark each practice that you complete each day.

⇒ Silence........................ ☐ M ☐ T ☐ W ☐ Th ☐ F ☐ S ☐ S
⇒ Affirmations............... ☐ M ☐ T ☐ W ☐ Th ☐ F ☐ S ☐ S
⇒ Visualization.............. ☐ M ☐ T ☐ W ☐ Th ☐ F ☐ S ☐ S
⇒ Exercise...................... ☐ M ☐ T ☐ W ☐ Th ☐ F ☐ S ☐ S
⇒ Reading....................... ☐ M ☐ T ☐ W ☐ Th ☐ F ☐ S ☐ S
⇒ Scribing...................... ☐ M ☐ T ☐ W ☐ Th ☐ F ☐ S ☐ S

Monday [____] – I will always find the best in others

_____

_____

_____

_____

_____

Tuesday [____] – I will leave the world a little bit better then when I entered it

_____

_____

_____

_____

_____

Wednesday [____] – I am what I choose to be

_____

_____

_____

_____

_____

Thursday [_____] – I am rewarded in direct proportion to my contribution

_____

_____

_____

_____

_____

_____

Friday [_____] – I will not make excuses, but instead, seek to learn from my mistakes

_____

_____

_____

_____

_____

Saturday [_____] – Each day will be my masterpiece

_____

_____

_____

_____

Sunday [_____] – I will give 100% of my focus to the person I am presently interacting with

_____

_____

_____

_____

_____

[Weekly Review] What were my accomplishments and disappointments? What commitments will I make NOW to ensure that I improve next week?

_____

_____

_____

_____

➜**Top Weekly Goals/Commitments** – The top 3-5 goals that I am 100% committed to achieving this week are:

_____
_____
_____
_____
_____

The Life S.A.V.E.R.S. Mark each practice that you complete each day.

		M	T	W	Th	F	S	S
⇒	Silence........................	☐	☐	☐	☐	☐	☐	☐
⇒	Affirmations..............	☐	☐	☐	☐	☐	☐	☐
⇒	Visualization..............	☐	☐	☐	☐	☐	☐	☐
⇒	Exercise......................	☐	☐	☐	☐	☐	☐	☐
⇒	Reading.......................	☐	☐	☐	☐	☐	☐	☐
⇒	Scribing......................	☐	☐	☐	☐	☐	☐	☐

Monday [_____] – I will embrace the challenge to do more

_____
_____
_____
_____
_____
_____

Tuesday [_____] – I love everyone including myself

_____
_____
_____
_____
_____
_____

Wednesday [_____] – I consciously think happy thoughts to be happy

_____
_____
_____
_____
_____
_____

Thursday [____] – I will face today with courage and enthusiasm

_____

_____

_____

_____

_____

_____

Friday [____] – I will be more successful with each day that passes

_____

_____

_____

_____

_____

_____

Saturday [____] – I will not forget those who have contributed to my success and I will find a way to thank them

_____

_____

_____

_____

_____

_____

Sunday [____] – I count my blessings instead of my problems

_____

_____

_____

_____

_____

_____

[Weekly Review] What were my accomplishments and disappointments? What commitments will I make NOW to ensure that I improve next week?

_____

_____

_____

_____

_____

_____

➜Top Weekly Goals/Commitments – The top 3-5 goals that I am 100% committed to achieving this week are:

_____

_____

_____

_____

_____

_____

The Life S.A.V.E.R.S. Mark each practice that you complete each day.
⇒ Silence............................ ☐ M ☐ T ☐ W ☐ Th ☐ F ☐ S ☐ S
⇒ Affirmations................ ☐ M ☐ T ☐ W ☐ Th ☐ F ☐ S ☐ S
⇒ Visualization............... ☐ M ☐ T ☐ W ☐ Th ☐ F ☐ S ☐ S
⇒ Exercise......................... ☐ M ☐ T ☐ W ☐ Th ☐ F ☐ S ☐ S
⇒ Reading.......................... ☐ M ☐ T ☐ W ☐ Th ☐ F ☐ S ☐ S
⇒ Scribing.......................... ☐ M ☐ T ☐ W ☐ Th ☐ F ☐ S ☐ S

Monday [____] – I will either find the way or create it

_____

_____

_____

_____

_____

Tuesday [____] – I am what I repeatedly do

_____

_____

_____

_____

_____

Wednesday [____] – I will do everything will all of my heart

_____

_____

_____

_____

_____

Thursday [____] – I will not wait to begin being happy. Today is that day

_____
_____
_____
_____
_____
_____

Friday [____] – I am always willing to try new things

_____
_____
_____
_____
_____
_____

Saturday [____] – Every single one of my beliefs is a choice

_____
_____
_____
_____
_____
_____

Sunday [____] – My positive thoughts will intensify with repetition

_____
_____
_____
_____
_____
_____

[Weekly Review] What were my accomplishments and disappointments? What commitments will I make NOW to ensure that I improve next week?

_____
_____
_____
_____
_____
_____

→**Top Weekly Goals/Commitments** – The top 3-5 goals that I am 100% committed to achieving this week are:

_____

_____

_____

_____

_____

The Life S.A.V.E.R.S. Mark each practice that you complete each day.

		M	T	W	Th	F	S	S
⇒	Silence............................	☐	☐	☐	☐	☐	☐	☐
⇒	Affirmations...............	☐	☐	☐	☐	☐	☐	☐
⇒	Visualization...............	☐	☐	☐	☐	☐	☐	☐
⇒	Exercise.........................	☐	☐	☐	☐	☐	☐	☐
⇒	Reading..........................	☐	☐	☐	☐	☐	☐	☐
⇒	Scribing.........................	☐	☐	☐	☐	☐	☐	☐

Monday [_____] – I am an admirable person, even when no one is looking

_____

_____

_____

_____

_____

Tuesday [_____] – I will accept anything that is beyond my control

_____

_____

_____

_____

_____

Wednesday [_____] – I never waste a good idea with inaction

_____

_____

_____

_____

_____

Thursday [_____] – When I encounter a challenge, I will not dwell on it, but begin searching for the solution

_____
_____
_____
_____
_____
_____

Friday [_____] – I will not limit my imagination when creating my dreams

_____
_____
_____
_____
_____
_____

Saturday [_____] – I will relish in the joy of sharing good news with others

_____
_____
_____
_____
_____
_____

Sunday [_____] – When I face a wall, I find a ladder

_____
_____
_____
_____
_____

[Weekly Review] What were my accomplishments and disappointments? What commitments will I make NOW to ensure that I improve next week?

_____
_____
_____
_____
_____

→**Top Weekly Goals/Commitments** – The top 3-5 goals that I am 100% committed to achieving this week are:

_____
_____
_____
_____
_____

The Life S.A.V.E.R.S. Mark each practice that you complete each day.

⇒ Silence............................ ☐ M ☐ T ☐ W ☐ Th ☐ F ☐ S ☐ S
⇒ Affirmations................. ☐ M ☐ T ☐ W ☐ Th ☐ F ☐ S ☐ S
⇒ Visualization................ ☐ M ☐ T ☐ W ☐ Th ☐ F ☐ S ☐ S
⇒ Exercise.......................... ☐ M ☐ T ☐ W ☐ Th ☐ F ☐ S ☐ S
⇒ Reading.......................... ☐ M ☐ T ☐ W ☐ Th ☐ F ☐ S ☐ S
⇒ Scribing.......................... ☐ M ☐ T ☐ W ☐ Th ☐ F ☐ S ☐ S

Monday [____] – What I believe in will become my experience

_____
_____
_____
_____
_____
_____

Tuesday [____] – Every positive action I take produces success

_____
_____
_____
_____
_____
_____

Wednesday [____] – I will never run out of ideas that excite and inspire me

_____
_____
_____
_____
_____
_____

Thursday [____] – I continually work to unleash the unending potential within me

_____

_____

_____

_____

_____

Friday [____] – I will wake up to find that my fantasies have become my life and the person I dreamed of becoming is my reflection in the mirror

_____

_____

_____

_____

_____

Saturday [____] – I believe in myself, therefore, everything is possible

_____

_____

_____

_____

_____

Sunday [____] – I will set goals as if I cannot fail

_____

_____

_____

_____

_____

[Weekly Review] What were my accomplishments and disappointments? What commitments will I make NOW to ensure that I improve next week?

_____

_____

_____

_____

_____

→**Top Weekly Goals/Commitments** – The top 3-5 goals that I am 100% committed to achieving this week are:

_____
_____
_____
_____
_____

The Life S.A.V.E.R.S. Mark each practice that you complete each day.

		M	T	W	Th	F	S	S
⇒	Silence	☐	☐	☐	☐	☐	☐	☐
⇒	Affirmations	☐	☐	☐	☐	☐	☐	☐
⇒	Visualization	☐	☐	☐	☐	☐	☐	☐
⇒	Exercise	☐	☐	☐	☐	☐	☐	☐
⇒	Reading	☐	☐	☐	☐	☐	☐	☐
⇒	Scribing	☐	☐	☐	☐	☐	☐	☐

Monday [____] – I will take my dreams seriously

_____
_____
_____
_____
_____

Tuesday [____] – I will never give up and I will not allow others to give up either

_____
_____
_____
_____
_____

Wednesday [____] – I will make big things happen a little at a time

_____
_____
_____
_____
_____

Thursday [____] – I see the beginning in every ending

_____

_____

_____

_____

_____

_____

Friday [____] – I inspire the best in others

_____

_____

_____

_____

_____

_____

Saturday [____] – I am rich in experience, laughter, and love

_____

_____

_____

_____

_____

_____

Sunday [____] – I look for the good and beautiful in everyone and every circumstance I encounter

_____

_____

_____

_____

_____

_____

[Weekly Review] What were my accomplishments and disappointments? What commitments will I make NOW to ensure that I improve next week?

_____

_____

_____

_____

_____

_____

→**Top Weekly Goals/Commitments** – The top 3-5 goals that I am 100% committed to achieving this week are:

_____

_____

_____

_____

_____

The Life S.A.V.E.R.S. Mark each practice that you complete each day.
⇒ Silence............................ ☐ M ☐ T ☐ W ☐ Th ☐ F ☐ S ☐ S
⇒ Affirmations............... ☐ M ☐ T ☐ W ☐ Th ☐ F ☐ S ☐ S
⇒ Visualization............... ☐ M ☐ T ☐ W ☐ Th ☐ F ☐ S ☐ S
⇒ Exercise........................ ☐ M ☐ T ☐ W ☐ Th ☐ F ☐ S ☐ S
⇒ Reading......................... ☐ M ☐ T ☐ W ☐ Th ☐ F ☐ S ☐ S
⇒ Scribing........................ ☐ M ☐ T ☐ W ☐ Th ☐ F ☐ S ☐ S

Monday [____] – I create win/win situations

_____

_____

_____

_____

_____

Tuesday [____] – I am sensitive to the needs of others

_____

_____

_____

_____

_____

Wednesday [____] – I motivate others by having faith in them

_____

_____

_____

_____

_____

— BONUS —
What You Must Do Now If You're Serious About Making the Next 12 Months Even Better.

Where's Your Focus Right Now?

As this year is near coming to a close, and next year just around the corner, what are you spending most of your time thinking about? Is it the upcoming holidays? Are you looking forward to spending time with family, taking a few days off of work, and getting some time to relax?

Or are you focused on the fast approaching new year, already thinking about strategizing what you're going to need to do *better* to make next year your best year yet? The opportunity to make next year the BEST YEAR OF YOUR LIFE is very real, although the question you must be able to answer is: are you *prepared* to make next year your best year yet? Unfortunately, most people are not.

Oh, I get it—you've heard this before. Maybe you're skeptical. Maybe you don't really believe it. Maybe there are some people reading this and thinking, "Yeah right, Hal. This year was *supposed* to be my best year ever, but it was far from that."

All too often, those of us with high standards and expectations for ourselves end the year feeling like we could have been so much better, and done and accomplished so much more. Some of us might feel like we failed. Some might feel discouraged. I think most of us are ready to learn from the past, put it behind us, and focus on creating our best year ever.

Is There Really a [Secret]?

There is one secret that you can put into action immediately, that will virtually guarantee that next year is by far, hands down, without-a-doubt the absolute BEST, most kick-butt, off-the-charts, life-changing year you've ever had!! But before we reveal this so called "secret" (which is really kind of a joke, since there are no secrets—only proven principles and strategies that, when applied to our lives, will give us the results, and the life, that we really want), let's look at why MOST people fail year-after-year, despite good intentions, to make each year significantly better than the previous.

Why People Fail:

Every year, around this time, we are focused primarily on two things: the *holidays* and the upcoming *New Year*. The problem with thinking about both of these simultaneously, is that they create very different, and almost conflicting mindsets. One is a time to relax and take it easy (the holidays) and the other is a time to get motivated and take massive action (the new year). Therein lies the problem; while people are gearing up for what they say they'd like to make their *best year ever*, they are creating and reinforcing an arsenal of bad habits that will be counterproductive to their success in the near year. Habits like *staying up late, over-sleeping, over-eating, being lazy, procrastinating*, choosing to do what *easy* over what's *right*, and many more that virtually destroy your chances of hitting the ground running on January 1st.

The [Secret] Revealed: What You Must Do NOW...

The truth is, that making next year your best year yet does NOT start January 1st. It starts TODAY. If you do what most people do and "check-out" for the next couple of weeks, creating and reinforcing an arsenal of unproductive habits, well then you're setting yourself up for failure next year. If you are really committed to making next year the best year you're ever had, you need to focus now on making the rest of December the best *month* you've ever created. You need to start living every day NOW the way you're going to need to live every day next year to make it your best, and not let the holidays become more detracting than a day to enjoy with your loved ones. You must start creating and reinforcing positive habits now and conditioning yourself mentally, emotionally, and physically to be the best version of yourself for the New Year. That is how you will guarantee your best next year.

YOU are destined for great things next year—things bigger and better than you have yet to even imagine! YOU are smart. YOU are capable. YOU are deserving. Huge opportunities are awaiting you this year, and if you give it everything you have, YOU cannot fail!

Sure, you'll stumble – we all will. We'll make mistakes and learn valuable lessons along the way, but failure is a mindset that isn't possible for those of us who continue moving forward and never give up! Decide to DO what you need to do, and more importantly—BE whom you're going to need to be to create your best next year.

If there is anything I can do to support your goals and dreams next year, send an email to hal@yopalhal.com.

Thursday [____] – I am open to new experiences and seek them out

_____

_____

_____

_____

_____

Friday [____] – I focus my thoughts and energy on what I want to achieve

_____

_____

_____

_____

_____

Saturday [____] – I am flexible and find ways to adjust to changes that come my way

_____

_____

_____

_____

_____

Sunday [____] – I tell myself I can until I believe that I can and then I tell myself again

_____

_____

_____

_____

_____

[Weekly Review] What were my accomplishments and disappointments? What commitments will I make NOW to ensure that I improve next week?

_____

_____

_____

_____

_____

➜Top Weekly Goals/Commitments – The top 3-5 goals that I am 100% committed to achieving this week are:

_____

_____

_____

_____

_____

The Life S.A.V.E.R.S. Mark each practice that you complete each day.

		M	T	W	Th	F	S	S
⇒	Silence	☐	☐	☐	☐	☐	☐	☐
⇒	Affirmations	☐	☐	☐	☐	☐	☐	☐
⇒	Visualization	☐	☐	☐	☐	☐	☐	☐
⇒	Exercise	☐	☐	☐	☐	☐	☐	☐
⇒	Reading	☐	☐	☐	☐	☐	☐	☐
⇒	Scribing	☐	☐	☐	☐	☐	☐	☐

Monday [____] – I focus on my strengths and how I can maximize them

_____

_____

_____

_____

_____

Tuesday [____] – Critics motivate me to prove them wrong

_____

_____

_____

_____

_____

Wednesday [____] – I will dream of things that do not exist yet, and find a way to bring them to life

_____

_____

_____

_____

_____

Thursday [____] – I thank everyone who makes my day go better

_____

_____

_____

_____

_____

Friday [____] – I let go of old ideas to make room for new ones

_____

_____

_____

_____

_____

Saturday [____] – I enjoy my responsibilities no matter what they are

_____

_____

_____

_____

_____

Sunday [____] – My success starts inside of me and permeates the world around me

_____

_____

_____

_____

_____

[Weekly Review] What were my accomplishments and disappointments? What commitments will I make NOW to ensure that I improve next week?

_____

_____

_____

_____

_____

→**Top Weekly Goals/Commitments** – The top 3-5 goals that I am 100% committed to achieving this week are:

_____
_____
_____
_____
_____

The Life S.A.V.E.R.S. Mark each practice that you complete each day.

⇒ Silence........................... ☐ M ☐ T ☐ W ☐ Th ☐ F ☐ S ☐ S
⇒ Affirmations............... ☐ M ☐ T ☐ W ☐ Th ☐ F ☐ S ☐ S
⇒ Visualization................ ☐ M ☐ T ☐ W ☐ Th ☐ F ☐ S ☐ S
⇒ Exercise........................ ☐ M ☐ T ☐ W ☐ Th ☐ F ☐ S ☐ S
⇒ Reading......................... ☐ M ☐ T ☐ W ☐ Th ☐ F ☐ S ☐ S
⇒ Scribing......................... ☐ M ☐ T ☐ W ☐ Th ☐ F ☐ S ☐ S

Monday [____] – I translate my visions into realities through my action

_____
_____
_____
_____
_____

Tuesday [____] – I give extraordinary effort and maintain unwavering faith

_____
_____
_____
_____
_____

Wednesday [____] – I inspire others into action by communicating my intentions authentically and from the heart

_____
_____
_____
_____
_____

Thursday [_____] – I bring out the best in others

_____

_____

_____

_____

_____

Friday [_____] – I judge each day not only by the end results, but by the effort and passion I invested in it

_____

_____

_____

_____

_____

Saturday [_____] – I embrace opportunities to serve others

_____

_____

_____

_____

_____

Sunday [_____] – I seek positive people and positive events to enhance my life

_____

_____

_____

_____

_____

[Weekly Review] What were my accomplishments and disappointments? What commitments will I make NOW to ensure that I improve next week?

_____

_____

_____

_____

_____

→**Top Weekly Goals/Commitments** – The top 3-5 goals that I am 100% committed to achieving this week are:

_____
_____
_____
_____
_____

The Life S.A.V.E.R.S. Mark each practice that you complete each day.

		M	T	W	Th	F	S	S
⇒	Silence............................	☐	☐	☐	☐	☐	☐	☐
⇒	Affirmations...............	☐	☐	☐	☐	☐	☐	☐
⇒	Visualization...............	☐	☐	☐	☐	☐	☐	☐
⇒	Exercise.........................	☐	☐	☐	☐	☐	☐	☐
⇒	Reading..........................	☐	☐	☐	☐	☐	☐	☐
⇒	Scribing.........................	☐	☐	☐	☐	☐	☐	☐

Monday [_____] – I will grow and move beyond my present circumstances

_____
_____
_____
_____
_____
_____

Tuesday [_____] – I will not wait for others to inspire me, I will begin to inspire myself

_____
_____
_____
_____
_____

Wednesday [_____] – I will be committed to my character

_____
_____
_____
_____
_____

Thursday [____] – My actions will always support my words

_____
_____
_____
_____
_____

Friday [____] – I will speak of my intentions with conviction

_____
_____
_____
_____
_____

Saturday [____] – I will believe in myself every second of every day

_____
_____
_____
_____
_____

Sunday [____] – I will do what I can with what I have, where I am, right now

_____
_____
_____
_____
_____

[Weekly Review] What were my accomplishments and disappointments? What commitments will I make NOW to ensure that I improve next week?

_____
_____
_____
_____
_____

➔**Top Weekly Goals/Commitments** – The top 3-5 goals that I am 100% committed to achieving this week are:

_____

_____

_____

_____

_____

The **Life S.A.V.E.R.S.** Mark each practice that you complete each day.

⇒ Silence............................	☐ M	☐ T	☐ W	☐ Th	☐ F	☐ S	☐ S
⇒ Affirmations..............	☐ M	☐ T	☐ W	☐ Th	☐ F	☐ S	☐ S
⇒ Visualization.............	☐ M	☐ T	☐ W	☐ Th	☐ F	☐ S	☐ S
⇒ Exercise......................	☐ M	☐ T	☐ W	☐ Th	☐ F	☐ S	☐ S
⇒ Reading.......................	☐ M	☐ T	☐ W	☐ Th	☐ F	☐ S	☐ S
⇒ Scribing......................	☐ M	☐ T	☐ W	☐ Th	☐ F	☐ S	☐ S

Monday [____] – I appreciate my family and love them for who they are

_____

_____

_____

_____

_____

Tuesday [____] – I am grateful for all that I have today

_____

_____

_____

_____

_____

Wednesday [____] – My life is a miracle

_____

_____

_____

_____

_____

Thursday [____] – I will live fully and savor every moment because life is lived in moments

_____

_____

_____

_____

_____

_____

Friday [____] – I am an optimist. The glass is always 100% full (half filled with abundance, and half filled with endless opportunities)

_____

_____

_____

_____

_____

_____

Saturday [____] – All challenges in my life pave my path to success

_____

_____

_____

_____

_____

_____

Sunday [____] – I expect good things

_____

_____

_____

_____

_____

_____

[Weekly Review] What were my accomplishments and disappointments? What commitments will I make NOW to ensure that I improve next week?

_____

_____

_____

_____

_____

_____

MONTH TWELVE (Week 52.5)

➜**Top Weekly Goals/Commitments** – The top 3-5 goals that I am 100% committed to achieving this week are:

_____

_____

_____

_____

_____

The Life S.A.V.E.R.S. Mark each practice that you complete each day.

⇒ Silence............................ ☐ M ☐ T ☐ W ☐ Th ☐ F ☐ S ☐ S
⇒ Affirmations................ ☐ M ☐ T ☐ W ☐ Th ☐ F ☐ S ☐ S
⇒ Visualization................. ☐ M ☐ T ☐ W ☐ Th ☐ F ☐ S ☐ S
⇒ Exercise........................... ☐ M ☐ T ☐ W ☐ Th ☐ F ☐ S ☐ S
⇒ Reading............................ ☐ M ☐ T ☐ W ☐ Th ☐ F ☐ S ☐ S
⇒ Scribing............................ ☐ M ☐ T ☐ W ☐ Th ☐ F ☐ S ☐ S

Monday [____] – I celebrate this year and am ready to make next year even better!

_____

_____

_____

_____

_____

_____

Tuesday [____] – Today is "My Best Year Ever's" Eve

_____

_____

_____

_____

_____

[Weekly Review] What were my accomplishments and disappointments? What commitments will I make NOW to ensure that I improve next week?

_____

_____

_____

_____

_____

```
┌─────────────────────────────────────┐
│                                     │
│   The Miracle MorningJournal        │
│   — ANNUAL REVIEW —                 │
│                                     │
└─────────────────────────────────────┘
```

Another miraculous year is behind us! Now is the ideal time to review your *Miracle Morning* Journal and evaluate your year by answering 4 simple, but powerful questions. This powerful process (which you already have experience with from doing your 6-MONTH REVIEW) will allow you to gain extraordinary value from this year by increasing your self-awareness, so that you can make adjustments and improvements to ensure that you take every area of your life to the next level next year.

Remember: this exercise is so important that I recommend scheduling a few hours to flip back to your first entry in your *Miracle Morning* Journal and relive your entire year as you come back to this page to answer the 4 "Best Year Ever" Questions below. Go ahead, and get started now. Or if now is not a good time, please put it in your schedule to do as soon as possible...

Your 4 "Best Year Ever" Questions To Ensure That the Next Year of Your Life Is the BEST Year of Your Life!

4 Questions to Take Your Life to the Next Level In the Next 6 Months:

Also remember that these four questions are SO valuable, the first time I did this exercise the answers I came up were so impactful that they inspired me to invest an entire weekend reflecting on my answers. (Note: you can answer these questions in 10 minutes or 10 hours, so don't feel like you *have* to spend the whole weekend on them, like I did.)

Here are your four "My Better Half" Questions, followed by a few specific action steps you can take in the next few days that will help you ensure that you implement the value you gain from this exercise:

1. What did I accomplish?
2. What were my biggest disappointments?
3. What valuable lessons can I learn from each?
4. What are my "Top 3" Guidelines for next year?

Q1 – What did I accomplish?

Unfortunately, most of us find it easier and tend to spend more time and energy dwelling on our failures and disappointments than we do acknowledging our successes and accomplishments. But all of us have *both*, and dwelling on our failures and what we 'didn't get accomplished' only discourages us and hurts our self-confidence.

It is only by acknowledging our accomplishments that we improve our self-image, raise our self-esteem, increase our self-confidence and empower ourselves to accomplish more in the future.

The first time I answered this questions, and wrote down as many of my accomplishments as I could think of (big ones & small ones) I got to 42, and the perception I had of the first half of my year started to change. I realized that I wasn't as behind as I had been telling myself I was. I gave myself permission to actually *feel good* about all that I accomplished. In fact, I even closed my eyes, smiled, and said to myself over and over, "You're doing great this year, Hal… You're doing great this year, Hal!" This may sound funny, but it felt so good to simply spend time acknowledging myself for once, for all that I had accomplished! Try it; I think you'll be pleasantly surprised by the results.

_____

_____

_____

_____

_____

_____

_____

_____

_____

_____

_____

_____

Q2 – What were my biggest disappointments?

While it is neither necessary nor particularly healthy to beat ourselves up about our disappointments, it IS important and proactive to acknowledge our disappointments so that we can learn from them and let them go. How did we let ourselves or others down last year? What goals did we fail to achieve? What bad habits did we continue?

160

Disappointments are a part of life, and we all have them. As long as we learn from our disappointments, we can use them to help us grow and improve so that we don't continue to make the in the future. As you review the first six months of this year, what were your biggest disappointments?

_____

_____

_____

_____

_____

_____

_____

_____

_____

_____

Q3 – What valuable lessons can I learn from each?

One lesson I have implemented that continues to empower me to improve every area of my life is to, *"Learn something from everything."* When it comes to learning from our 'accomplishments' we can take away valuable lessons related to what it was that motivated, inspired, or allowed us to accomplish what we accomplished. As for learning from our disappointments, we can internalize valuable lessons about which thoughts, behaviors, actions, emotions, or habits prompted us to create or to not create that which disappointed us. Usually it is our biggest disappointments that can provide us with our most life-changing lessons.

_____

_____

_____

_____

_____

_____

_____

_____

_____

_____

Q4 – What are my "Top 3" Success Guidelines for the next 6 months?

One you have acknowledged your accomplishments and your disappointments, and you've extracted the most valuable, life-enhancing LESSONS from each, what may benefit you the most is choosing your "Top 3" guidelines to keep you on track during the coming year. You can simply copy and paste your 3 most empowering lessons, and post these up somewhere that you will look at them every day to stay focused on that which will make the biggest impact on improving your life next year and beyond.

Here are the Top 3 Success Guidelines that I came up with in 2008:

1. Focus on one project (or task) at a time and complete it, before moving onto the next.
2. Delegate all tasks that don't compliment my natural gifts and unique areas of brilliance.
3. Make everything I do FUN and done with unconditional LOVE and authentic GRATITUDE.

So, what are your top 3 Success Guidelines for the next 6 months?

1. _____
   _____
   _____

2. _____
   _____
   _____

3. _____
   _____
   _____

Closing Thoughts: Congratulations on completing your first year of documenting your life's journey in *The Miracle Morning* JOURNAL. I wish you extraordinary happiness, health, and success in all that you do.

➔ **Order Next Year's Miracle Morning Journal at**
MiracleMorningJournal.com

Praise for The Miracle Morning (Book)

⇒ Get 2 FREE Chapters (or let your friends and family know) at
www.MiracleMorning.com

"The Miracle Morning is literally the ONE thing that will make immediate and profound changes in any—or *every* area of your life. If you really want your life to improve, read this book immediately."
—RUDY RUETTIGER, the Notre Dame football player
who inspired the hit Hollywood movie *RUDY*

"Every once in a while, you read a book that changes the way you look at life. But it is so rare to find a book that changes the way you *live* your life. *The Miracle Morning* does both, and faster than you ever thought possible. I highly recommend Hal Elrod's latest book."
—TIM SANDERS, NY Times bestselling author of *The Likability Factor*

"At first I thought Hal had lost his mind—why on earth would anyone get up so early *on a regular basis*?! I was skeptical... until I tried it. When I implemented Hal's strategies I noticed an immediate difference in my personal and professional life. *The Miracle Morning* shows you how to take control of your life, regardless of your past. I highly recommend it."
—JOSH SHIPP, TV show host, author, and teen behavior expert

"To read *The Miracle Morning* is to give yourself the gift of waking up each day to your full potential. It's time to stop putting off creating the life you want, and deserve to live. Read this book and find out how."
—DR. IVAN MISNER, NY Times bestselling author and Founder of BNI®

"I love Hal Elrod. He is a powerful teacher, and a man of great insight and high integrity. Reading his first book, *Taking Life Head On!* completely changed the way I live each day, and I've been waiting patiently for his next book. All I can say is that *The Miracle Morning* was definitely worth the wait. Hal gives us the blueprint for creating the success, happiness and prosperity that may be have eluded us, and he's made it so simple that anyone can turn their life around—no matter what their circumstances."
—DEBRA PONEMAN, Co-author of *Chicken Soup for the*
American Idol® Soul and Founder of Yes to Success, Inc.

Made in the USA
Columbia, SC
14 May 2021

37943556R00095